D0848802

About the TLS

The *Times Literary Supplement* was born in January 1902. Its first ever front page bashfully stated that 'during the Parliamentary session Literary Supplements to "The Times" will appear as often as may be necessary in order to keep abreast with the more important publications of the day'. Fortunately, the question of necessity was not left in the hands of literary journalists (who, we can imagine, might occasionally push for a holiday or two), and the title became a weekly one. A few years later, the *TLS* split entirely from *The Times*.

Since then, we have prided ourselves on being the world's leading magazine for culture and ideas. Our guiding principle for the selection of pieces remains the same as it ever has been: is it interesting; and is it beautifully written? Over the years, our contributors have included the very best writers and thinkers in the world: from Virginia Woolf to Seamus Heaney, Sylvia Plath to Susan Sontag, Milan Kundera to Christopher Hitchens, Patricia Highsmith to Martin Scorsese.

The book you are holding is part of a brand-new imprint, *TLS Books*, by which we are striving to bring more beautiful writing to a wider public. We hope you enjoy it. If you want to read more from us, you'll find a special trial subscription offer to the *TLS* at the back of this book.

In an ever-quickening culture of flipness and facility, fake news and Facebook, the *TLS* is determined to be part of the counter-culture of quality. We believe in expertise, breadth and depth. We believe in the importance of ideas, and the transformative power of art. And we believe that, in reading the *TLS* – in whatever form, be it in a magazine, online or in a book – you are supporting a set of values that we have been proud to uphold for more than a hundred years. So thank you for that.

Stig Abell, 11th Editor of the *TLS*
London, 2019

Genius and Ink

Works by Virginia Woolf

Genius and Ink

*Virginia Woolf
on How to Read*

TLS

TLS Books
An imprint of HarperCollins*Publishers*
1 London Bridge Street
London SE1 9GF

The-TLS.co.uk

First published in Great Britain in 2019 by TLS Books

19 20 21 22 LSC 10 9 8 7 6 5 4 3 2

A catalogue record for this book is
available from the British Library

ISBN 978-0-00-835572-2

Typeset in Publico Text
Printed and bound in the United States of America by
LSC Communications

For more information visit· www.harpercollins.co.uk/green

Two things I mean to do when the long dark evenings come: to write, on the spur of the moment, as now, lots of little poems to go into *P.H.*: as they may come in handy: to collect, even bind together, my innumerable *T.L.S.* notes: to consider them as material for some kind of critical book: quotations? comments? ranging all through English literature as I've read it and noted it during the past 20 years.

Virginia Woolf, 1938

Contents

Preface

By Ali Smith

Genius and ink: the phrase that gives this book its title has been notched out of 'On Re-reading Novels', one of the essays by Virginia Woolf written over two decades as a reviewer and critic for the *Times Literary Supplement*. Ostensibly a consideration of Percy Lubbock's 1921 publication *The Craft of Fiction*, the real focus of 'On Re-reading Novels' is the beginnings of the critical attempt towards a fuller understanding of the novel as form. Woolf wrote it at a time when ideas about the shape of the novel were about to defy all former imaginings. James Joyce's *Ulysses* had been serialized and passed around in bits and pieces for the preceding four years and was finally published in its entirety in early 1922; and Woolf's own transformatory work had begun with her first truly great experimental novel *Jacob's Room*, which she published three months after this essay appeared. You might say the whole notion of what a novel could be was being re-read.

So what makes a novel a novel, then? 'Obviously there must be a process, and it is at work always and in every novel', she writes in July 1922. 'We must have been aware that a novelist, before he can persuade us that his world is real and his people alive, must solve certain questions and acquire certain skill. But until Mr. Lubbock pierced through the flesh and made us look at the skeleton we were almost ready to believe that nothing was needed but genius and ink.' Thank you, Mr. L, she says, for the helpful attention paid to the concept of process, meanwhile she quietly infers that his splaying-open of the form is also a kind of killing.

When it comes to literary form and its relation to concepts of reality, or concepts of literary/literal aliveness in the form of the novel, Woolf would ask something a lot more vital from critical response. This collection lets its readers trace the formation of her own critical voice, through her responses to a range of classic (and not so classic) writers and literary forms. It charts a timeline of pieces via which her open, wry and intuitive reading of a work or a writer shifts in potency from an early brilliance that's conscious of (and still a bit beholden to) deference to tradition, to the finding of a formidable vital intelligence of voice and critical form, one which would revolutionize the possibilities of critical writing.

She complains repeatedly in her diaries about how little she gets paid for it, but she clearly loved writing for the *TLS*. She also habitually, playfully, always fruitfully, tended to baulk against or question notions of establishment and authority, especially literary establishment, so it's no surprise to find her in her diaries yo-yoing between feeling 'important & even excited' at being sent something to review, and by turn dejected, 'rejected', when no books from the *Times* arrive, though this 'has the result of making me write my novel at an astonishing rate. If I continue dismissed, I shall finish within a month or two'. But Woolf was also one of the earliest critics actively to defy the preconception of a divide between what's called critical and what's called creative writing. In her, the revolutionary novelist is still the critic, the revolutionary critic will always also be the novelist, and this open symbiosis makes for a body of work that ensures the imaginative vitality of both. She'll invest critique with narrative. Her narrative will never not, one way or another, involve or ask critique.

As for the real, the flesh, the bones of the literary: every essay collected here relates literary nature to the larger concept of nature in the real world. What 'real works of art' have in common, she suggests, is that each has 'some change in them' with every 'fresh reading ... as if the sap of life ran in their leaves, and with skies and plants they had the power to alter their shape and colour from season to season'.

This particular natural conjunction turns up in 'Charlotte Brontë' (1916), the earliest essay collected here and a gentle, reasonably knee-bending though still sharp and intuitive piece (noting the 'crudeness', the 'violence' in Brontë's work and the simultaneous force of 'compulsion' in it, the 'gesture of defiance'), an essay written by a writer still new to the novel form herself, with *The Voyage Out* already published and the workings of *Night and Day* in progress. Just four years later, by the time of her coruscating and irrepressible extended critique of the novels of Henry James, Woolf has become not just a writer about to produce, herself, a new kind of fiction, but a markedly new kind of critic too, an eyebrow-raiser, a risk-taker. She senses the uses of repression in James's narrative. She senses the unsaid, and says so – senses the 'secret of it all' in the writer who's 'shut himself up', who's 'surrounded himself with furniture of the right period'. She proceeds not just to pin but merrily to skewer James the butterfly, 'unattached, uncommitted, ranging hither and thither at his own free will, and only at length precariously settling and delicately inserting his proboscis in the thickset lusty blossoms of the old garden beds'. It's like a wink to camera. 'One admits a momentary malice.' Her James essay is a piece of pure mischief – full of generosity all the same, ending as it does on an extraordinary garlanding.

Wry, warm, funny, blatant only in the sheer blatancy of its intelligence, close to (but never outright) scornful and always in the end leaving room for readers to disagree or feel differently, what her style asks and expects of us is an equally applied intelligence. Woolf the critic is a forgiving reader as well as one happy to puncture the over-inflated, to point out when something's not working or falls short. She never short-changes what she's critiquing and she never short-changes the act of critique. She knows in her own bones how important a generous, open reading is, especially when it comes to the difficult critiquing of 'the people who are giving shape as best they can to the ideas within them', the contemporary writers, the hardest to judge, of which she's one, 'casting their net out over some unknown abyss to snare new shapes ... we must throw our imaginations after them if we are to accept with understanding the strange gifts they bring back to us'.

Stylistically, she is herself a dredger-up of gifts. She is unique in voice, even while her immersion in a writer's writing simultaneously produces a kind of knowing ventriloquism, so that the writer or writing being channelled and unmasked through Woolf has nowhere to hide. Is it the vitality of her intuition or the perfect pitch of her literary ear, formed by a life of wide, anarchic, studied reading, that gives her one of her great gifts, an uncanny, poetically resonant use of conjunction? The 'word-coining genius' of the Elizabethan dramatists strikes her 'as if thought plunged into a sea of words and came up dripping'. She hears in Thomas Hardy's writing the workings of a resonance that's subconscious even to him, as if 'very far away, like the sound of a gun out at sea on a calm summer's morning'.

Above all, this collection reveals Woolf's preoccupation with how to make a story – whether memoir, drama, fiction – both true to life and truly alive. This is a preoccupation which resonates socially, politically and aesthetically throughout her writing life, through all her chosen forms and her transformations of them. Take her re-evaluation of Elizabeth Barrett Browning's *Aurora Leigh*: while it admits the poem's problems and applauds as a sign of real life even the failure in Barrett Browning's attempt to bring poetry and her contemporary world together into a working form, it also nails literary snobbery in a critiquing of the kind of literary classism which had demoted Barrett Browning 'to the servants' quarters' along with a bunch of other writers rejected for being old fashioned or unacceptable. It's also an essay fully aware of historical gender constraints, and one in which readers can trace the fruit of the recently published *A Room of One's Own* and the root of the not-yet-written *Flush*; because this collection also gifts its readers the pleasure of encountering, in embryo or aftermath, the books on which Woolf has been working and the books on which she will shortly embark.

Here in the form of essays, written for not-enough-money, when the newspaper deigned to send a book or ask an appraisal, is the response of the imagination to the place where the real and the imaginative meet. Even if what she ends up reading is 'as much out of harmony with imagination as a bedroom cupboard is with the dream of someone waking from sleep' ('The Captain's Death Bed'), Woolf is a writer for whom, for instance, in *To the Lighthouse*, a mere cupboard, with some drinking glasses in it which suddenly clink together for what seems no fathomable reason, marks a reverberation so far away that it hardly registers on human consciousness but will all the same shake us to the core, will mean a world war, a great and terrible loss, a momentous understanding. This is a writer for whom everything is invested with life and death and the imagination it takes to read and write both.

When I finished reading this collection, I found myself wanting to go and read or re-read everything she'd read and written about here. That's surely the whole point. 'A great critic, they say, is the rarest of beings. But should one miraculously appear, how should we maintain him, on what should we feed him?' On the writings of Woolf, of course, in all its forms: flesh, bones, genius, ink.

Introduction

By Francesca Wade

I do not care about writing introductions – to me a
very difficult proceeding ...
Virginia Woolf, 1932

When, in May 1938, Bruce Richmond retired as Editor of
the *Times Literary Supplement,* Virginia Woolf noted in
her diary her sadness at ending her '30 year connection'
with him and the 'Lit Supp'. Richmond had sent her
hundreds of books for review, each time receiving back a
dazzling critique which might cast a familiar writer in
entirely fresh light or offer a provocative manifesto for
what fiction or biography could become. His early
support of her writing offered Woolf her first experience
of financial independence, while the ideas she developed
in these pieces – on the possibilities of language, character and style; on the importance of life-writing and the
limitations of gender – seeped directly into her greatest
fiction and essays. Although they had never established
much of a personal friendship, she reflected now that

Richmond had been one of the most influential figures in her life. 'How pleased I used to be', she recalled, 'when L. called me "You're wanted by the Major Journal!" & I ran down to the telephone to take my almost weekly orders at Hogarth House! I learnt a lot of my craft writing for him: how to compress; how to enliven; & also was made to read with a pen & notebook, seriously.'

Woolf met Richmond in February 1905, following a turbulent year in her life. On February 22, 1904, her father Leslie Stephen – whose regular rages, borne of grief at his wife's premature death, had instilled dread into his daughters – had died. In the following months she experienced a traumatic breakdown, and moved with her siblings from their Kensington family home to 46 Gordon Square in Bloomsbury, seeking a 'new beginning'. There, Virginia was no longer forced to perform the drawing-room pageantry of serving tea to her father's eminent friends, but had her own private sitting-room in which to read and write, while downstairs mixed groups of friends lounged into the early hours, casually discussing philosophy, art and sex over whisky or cocoa. And this shift in domestic arrangement heralded a significant development in her public life. In December 1904, following the encouragement of a family friend, her first short article was published in a clerical women's weekly, confusingly called *The Guardian*. Two months later, at a party, she was introduced to Bruce Richmond ('a restless vivacious little man, jumping onto a chair to see the traffic over the blind, & chivvying a piece of paper round the room with his feet'). Richmond had been appointed editor of the *Times Literary Supplement* shortly after its foundation in 1902 as an eight-page cultural appendage to *The Times*. Under his aegis, its weekly circulation had already reached 20,000, and it was widely acknowledged (in the words of T. S. Eliot, a regular contributor) as 'the most respected and most respectable' literary periodical of its day. Richmond invited Woolf to submit 1,500 words on a couple of 'trashy' guidebooks to Thackeray's and Dickens's England. The books, she disdainfully insisted, seemed 'the productions of a pair of scissors'; nonetheless, she worked 'like the little Printers devil I am' to complete the piece and dispatch it to Richmond within days. Her review was published on March 10, and soon Woolf gloated that she had received 'another book from the *Times*! – a fat novel, I'm sorry to say. They pelt me now'. Aged twenty-three, Woolf was now a writer, earning money by her pen as her father had before her. Her wage-slip arrived with her breakfast plate. 'Now we are free women', she declared triumphantly.

In her 1931 essay 'Professions for Women', Woolf recalled that thrill of transforming from 'a girl in a bedroom with a pen in her hand' to 'a professional woman', her opinions solicited and rewarded by wages she could spend, once rent and bills were covered, on 'an extravagant little table' or a 'long coveted & resisted coal scuttle' (money, she wrote in *A Room of One's Own*, 'dignifies what is frivolous if unpaid for'). But the sense of independence afforded by this work was not purely, or even primarily, financial. When she first sat down to write a damning review of a book by a respected gentleman, Woolf was haunted by a phantom voice urging her not to criticize but to charm and flatter, to speak in the language traditionally deemed womanly. She named this spectre the 'Angel in the House', after Coventry Patmore's poem about the cloying, self-sacrificing ideal of Victorian womanhood; her imagined admonishment – 'Never let anybody guess that you have a mind of your own' – nearly 'plucked the heart out of my writing'. Conquering the urge to submit to that voice, Woolf concluded, was a prerequisite not only for writing, but for freedom in all aspects of life. The *TLS*'s affirmation helped Woolf to unmake assumptions of how women should think and behave, and find a new language in which to express herself, ignoring the insistent reminder that there were things 'which it was unfitting for her as a woman to say'. Soon after her first reviews were published, seeking respite from dull commissions ('a nondescript book like this which really suggests nothing good or bad, is damned hard work'), she began on the novel that would become her debut, *The Voyage Out*. Virginia Woolf was launched.

All reviews that appeared in the *TLS* were published anonymously (a practice that continued until 1974). This meant that Woolf didn't have to fear public disapproval for her forthright views, but rather was invited to speak as part of a collective authority, assuming an expertise conferred by dint of the periodical's prestige. Though she enjoyed experimenting subversively with the power afforded by that universal 'we', Woolf believed essays should always be firmly rooted in their authors' 'personal peculiarities', and aimed from the very beginning to find and develop her own distinctive voice: to 'say what I thought, & say it in my own way'. She never set out to provide an impersonal, authoritative assessment of a work or author, but something ostensibly humble, yet in fact radical and generous: to 'offer merely our little hoard of observations, which other readers may like to set, for a moment, beside their own'. She had no interest in respectable hagiography or regurgitation of received opinion: for Woolf, a book's interest lay in the feelings it stirred in its reader, which would inevitably – crucially – be entirely personal and subjective. Her role, as she saw it, was to share her own enthusiasms with her audience, to acknowledge and celebrate the influence of her own 'cranks', tastes and interests as she guided them 'to enter into the mind of the writer; to see each work of art by itself, and to judge how far each artist has succeeded in his aim'. Her loyalty always remained with her audience, whom she imagined as 'busy people catching trains in the morning or ... tired people coming home in the evening'; when she came to collect her reviews and essays into a book, in 1925, she called it *The Common Reader* (borrowing a phrase from Samuel Johnson).

She was not averse to the occasional hatchet-job ('my real delight in reviewing is to say nasty things', she once wrote), but she insisted that 'praise ought to have the last word and the weightiest'. This was not to be saccharine – she despaired that most reviews were 'too short and too positive' – but enthusiasm, she wrote, is 'the life-blood of criticism'. Her own reviewing, she mused in her diary, was an act of 'testifying before I die to the great fun & pleasure my habit of reading has given me'. Her evident joy courses irresistibly through these pieces. Woolf's writing imparts a remarkable sense of how it *feels* to read: her exhilaration on closing *Jane Eyre* and feeling 'that we have parted from a most singular and eloquent woman, met by chance upon a Yorkshire hillside, who has gone with us for a time and told us the whole of her life history'; her conviction, on reading John Evelyn's diary, that his staid remarks were a flawed attempt to conceal a far richer, more acerbic and deeply insecure psyche. As an essayist, Woolf's erudite, conversational style can be traced back through Montaigne, Charles Lamb, Max Beerbohm and Walter Pater, yet every piece is an utterly original distillation of her personality, wit and intellect.

'You cast a beam across the dingy landscape of the *Times Literary Supplement*', wrote Vita Sackville-West to Woolf, in the course of enumerating her lover's most seductive qualities. No other writer would compare the experience of reading Joseph Conrad to that of Helen of Troy gazing into a mirror, sensing instantly that she was in the presence of greatness; who else would think to tell the life of naval officer-turned-novelist Captain Marryat through a series of open questions at least as engaging as any answers might be, thus revealing 'one of the most active, odd and adventurous lives that any English novelist has ever lived'. Woolf's work for the *TLS* provided a stage for her lifelong engagement with the problems and potentials of biography: she had welcomed the rise of the 'new biography' amid the social freedoms of the new century, which swapped lifeless panegyric for shorter, more self-aware studies, and these pieces form some of her most compelling miniature experiments in the form. She was never interested in mining works for straightforward biographical details, but sought to draw out hints at her subjects' inner lives, through deeply sympathetic attention to the nuances of texture and atmosphere. Her character studies are imbued with the insatiable curiosity of a gossip, the insight of a novelist and the steely intellect of a great critic, whether she is imagining the young Fanny Burney and her stepsister confiding at night their secret passions, pondering whether our views on love and pain have changed since John Evelyn's time, or lamenting the stereotype of the 'bookish man': 'a pale, attenuated figure in a dressing gown, lost in speculation, unable to lift a kettle from the hob, or address a lady without blushing, ignorant of the daily news, though versed in the catalogues of the secondhand booksellers, in whose dark premises he spends the hours of sunlight'.

Bruce Richmond quickly came to consider Woolf his jewel in a cohort of reviewers that included T. S. Eliot, Henry James, Edith Wharton, George Gissing and Andrew Lang. In November 1905, Woolf breezily told a friend that the *TLS* 'sends me one novel every week; which has to be read on Sunday, written on Monday, and printed on Friday. In America, as you know, they make sausages like that.' She loved the rhythm and routine of these assignments: the feeling of alchemy as an essay 'expands under my hands', the satisfaction of hearing that a respected editor was 'delighted to accept my charming article', the excitement, on occasion, of visiting Richmond himself at the *TLS* office in Printing House Square, breezing past carts waiting to transport fresh bales of papers to the newsagents ('carrying my manuscript to the *Times* I felt like a hack much in keeping'). At other times, when she was up against her deadline, it was an even greater frisson to find that the *TLS* would come to her:

> I write & write; I am rung up & told to stop writing; review must be had on Friday; I typewrite till the messenger from the *Times* appears; I correct the pages in my bedroom with him sitting over the fire here.
>
> 'A Christmas number not at all to Mr Richmond's taste,' he said. 'Very unlike the supplement style.'
>
> 'Gift books, I suppose?' I suggested.
>
> 'O no, Mrs Woolf, it's for the advertisers.'

At first, she reviewed anything Richmond tossed her, covering cookery books and travel guides, poetry and swathes of debut novels. But in 1920, exhausted by the commitment, she decided to dictate her own terms – 'only leading articles, or those I suggest myself' – and felt a triumphant release 'like a drunkard who has success-fully resisted three invitations to drink'. Even when she was writing only on subjects she had chosen, she some-times resented having to compromise with an editor: when Richmond reprimanded her for calling Henry James 'lewd' ('Now poor dear old Henry James – at any rate, think it over, & ring me up in 20 minutes'), she resolved furiously to work with no one who 'rewrites my sentences to suit the mealy mouths of Belgravia'. She wondered anxiously whether the best form of criticism was that spoken 'over wine glasses and coffee cups late at night'. But Woolf never stopped writing for the *TLS*, even after she became established as a novelist and publisher and began to complain in her diary at the drudgery of '1,500 words by Wednesday' which eroded the time she had for other writing. The *TLS* was far too integral a part of her life as a writer for her to abandon its pages. Across these decades, it provided a crucial testing-ground for radical new ideas; the books she wrote on, the authors she examined, became Woolf's personal canon.

Each of these pieces is a gem in its own right, and deserves to be read purely for itself. Yet it is also fascinating to read these essays in conjunction with Woolf's other work, to trace the way she grappled across projects with knotty existential questions and put her principles into practice. While she was stuck on her 1919 novel *Night and Day*, feeling frustrated at her inability to eschew the confines of realism, she was busy analysing the state of postwar fiction and calling for 'new forms for our new sensations'. By the time she published 'How It Strikes a Contemporary', her great assessment of the stakes for literature in 'an age of fragments', she had completed *Jacob's Room*, her formal breakthrough, and was looking ahead to *Mrs Dalloway* and *To the Lighthouse*, in which she would address the present upheaval through her experiments with structure and language. In January 1919, she began 'reading through the whole of George Eliot, in order to sum her up, once and for all, upon her anniversary'; that same year she opened a fresh notebook to gather her thoughts on her father's friend Thomas Hardy, in response to a request from Richmond to 'be ready with an article on Hardy's novels whenever the evil day comes'. She worked sporadically on the piece ('Thomas Hardy's Novels') for the next ten years. 'I pray he sits safe & sound by his fireside at this moment', she wrote guiltily in December 1921, having failed to finish a new draft; it was eventually published on his death in 1928. Her ongoing attempt 'to discover the broad outlines of his genius' was the backdrop to all her work in this formative decade.

But of all Woolf's books, it is perhaps *A Room of One's Own* (1929) that bears the closest relationship with her *TLS* reviews. Her sparkling essays on Charlotte Brontë, George Eliot and Elizabeth Barrett Browning are rich case studies in that book's major theme: the way women's lives have been, throughout history, narrowed and curtailed by pernicious social expectations. Barrett Browning's early life shared certain features with Woolf's own: the early deaths of a mother and beloved brother, periods of illness, a tyrannical father, and an ability to take comfort in reading 'profusely and privately', using books as 'a substitute for living'. Woolf's sympathy is palpable when she describes Barrett Browning locked in her bedroom engrossed in stories of 'immortal improprieties', starved of conversation or intellectual impetus. The essay 'Aurora Leigh' is a powerful denunciation of what it means for anyone to be forced to live inside their own mind, rather than out in the world:

> She raced through folios because she was forbidden to scamper on the grass. She wrestled with Aeschylus and Plato because it was out of the question that she should argue about politics with live men and women ... It cannot be doubted that the long years of seclusion had done her irreparable damage as an artist. She had lived shut off, guessing at what was outside, and inevitably magnifying what was within.

Browning's poem *Aurora Leigh*, Woolf concludes, is 'a masterpiece in embryo': 'a work whose genius floats diffused and fluctuating in some pre-natal stage waiting the final stroke of creative power to bring it into being'.

A Room of One's Own was published thirteen years after Woolf's *TLS* piece on Charlotte Brontë, a decade after that on George Eliot, but its citation of both writers as powerful examples of astonishing female creativity nonetheless circumscribed by social norms is testament to Woolf's long, ongoing engagement with their work, sparked decisively in these early reviews. She planned to return to this theme in her final project, begun in autumn 1940 as bomber planes soared over her Sussex home. This was to be an idiosyncratic history of English popular culture, in which Woolf intended to examine not only 'the germ of creation' in writers but also the social forces that stymied imagination. Her insistence that a work cannot be understood without knowledge of the circumstances of its creation was the defining feature of her scheme, extending the principles she had developed in her biographical essays to the story of literature, and of England, in its entirety. The project was the triumphant culmination of decades of research, languishing within her 'innumerable *TLS* notes': in the surviving synopsis lie the vestiges of the year she spent devouring Elizabethan playwrights, her insatiable fascination with 'obscure lives', her belief in the importance of an intimate relationship between artist and audience. That work – sure to have been artful, esoteric and radical – was never finished, but these essays reveal the contours of all that might have been.

Books, Woolf insisted, come alive on encountering a reader, and change with them. Our impressions of the same book across a lifetime, she wrote, could form our own autobiography: art can only survive if new generations discover it afresh and find new pleasure in it. Woolf's reviews richly deserve to be celebrated as works of literature worth reading and re-reading in themselves. But once this book is finished, she sends us back to the shelves, eager to see what she saw, and to discover what we feel for ourselves.

Genius
and Ink

Charlotte Brontë

The hundredth anniversary of the birth of Charlotte Brontë will strike, we believe, with peculiar force upon the minds of a very large number of people. Of those hundred years she lived but thirty-nine, and it is strange to reflect what a different image we might have of her if her life had been a long one. She might have become, like other writers who were her contemporaries, a figure familiarly met with in London and elsewhere, the subject of anecdotes and pictures innumerable, removed from us well within the memory of the middle-aged, in all the splendour of established fame. But it is not so. When we think of her we have to imagine some one who had no lot in our modern world; we have to cast our minds back to the fifties of the last century, to a remote parsonage upon the wild Yorkshire moors. Very few now are those who saw her and spoke to her; and her posthumous reputation has not been prolonged by any circle of friends whose memories so often keep alive for a new generation the most vivid and most perishable characteristics of a dead man.

Nevertheless, when her name is mentioned, there starts up before our eyes a picture of Charlotte Brontë, which is as definite as that of a living person, and one may venture to say that to place her name at the head of a page will cause a more genuine interest than almost any other inscription that might be placed there. What new thing, one may well ask, is to be said of so strange and famous a being? How can we add anything about her life or her work which is not already part of the consciousness of the educated man and woman of today? We have seen Haworth, either in fact or in picture; long ago Mrs. Gaskell stamped our minds with an ineffaceable impression; and the devotion of later students has swept together every trifle that may render back the echoes of that short and circumscribed life.

But there is one peculiarity which real works of art possess in common. At each fresh reading one notices some change in them, as if the sap of life ran in their leaves, and with skies and plants they had the power to alter their shape and colour from season to season. To write down one's impressions of *Hamlet* as one reads it year after year, would be virtually to record one's own autobiography, for as we know more of life, so Shakespeare comments upon what we know. In their degree, the novels of Charlotte Brontë must be placed within the same class of living and changing creations, which so far as we can guess, will serve a generation yet unborn with a glass in which to measure its varying stature. In their turn they will say how she has changed to them, and what she has given them. If we collect a few of our impressions today, it is not with any hope of assigning her to her final position, or of drawing her portrait afresh; we offer merely our little hoard of observations, which other readers may like to set, for a moment, beside their own.

So many novels once held great have gone out of fashion, or are pronounced unreadable, that we may justly feel a little anxiety when the time comes to make trial of *Jane Eyre* and the rest. We have suggested that a book, in order to live, must have the power of changing as we change, and we have to ask ourselves whether it is possible that Charlotte Brontë can have kept pace with us. Shall we not go back to her world of the fifties and find that it is a place only to be visited by the learned, only to be preserved for the curious? A novelist, we reflect, is bound to build up his structure with much very perishable material, which begins by lending it reality, and ends by cumbering its form. The mid-Victorian world, moreover, is the last that we of the present moment wish to see resuscitated. One opens *Jane Eyre* with all these half-conscious premonitions and excuses, and in ten minutes one finds the whole of them dispersed and the light shining and the wind blowing upon a wild and bracing prospect.

Folds of scarlet drapery shut in my view to the right hand; to the left were the clear panes of glass, protecting, but not separating, me from the drear November day. At intervals while turning over the leaves of my book, I studied the aspects of that winter afternoon. Afar, it offered a pale blank of mist and cloud; near, a scene of wet lawn and storm-beat shrub, with ceaseless rain sweeping away wildly before a long and lamentable blast.

As a room full of people makes one who enters suddenly conscious of heightened existence, so the opening passages of this book make us glow and shiver as though we stood out in the storm and saw the rain drive across the moor. There is nothing here that seems more perishable than the moor itself, or more subject to the sway of fashion than the 'long and lamentable blast'. Nor is this exhilaration short-lived; it rushes us through the entire volume and scarcely gives us time to ask what is happening to us, nor in the end are we able to make out a very clear account of our adventures. We may reflect that this is exactly the opposite of our experience with certain other books justly numbered among the great. When we have finished *The Idiot* or *Jude the Obscure*, and even in the course of reading them, the plethoric state of mind which they induce is to be traced in a head resting on the hands, and oblivious eyes fixed upon the fire. We brood and ponder and drift away from the text in trains of thought which build up round the characters an atmosphere of question and suggestion in which they move, but of which they are unconscious. But it is not possible, when you are reading Charlotte Brontë, to lift your eyes from the page. She has you by the hand and forces you along her road, seeing the things she sees and as she sees them. She is never absent for a moment, nor does she attempt to conceal herself or to disguise her voice. At the conclusion of *Jane Eyre* we do not feel so much that we have read a book, as that we have parted from a most singular and eloquent woman, met by chance upon a Yorkshire hillside, who has gone with us for a time and told us the whole of her life history. So strong is the impression that if we are disturbed while we are reading the disturbance seems to take place in the novel and not in the room.

There are two reasons for this astonishing closeness and sense of personality – that she is herself the heroine of her own novels, and (if we may divide people into those who think and those who feel) that she is primarily the recorder of feelings and not of thoughts. Her characters are linked together by their passions as by a train of gunpowder. One of these small, pale, volcanic women, be she Jane Eyre or Lucy Snowe, has but to come upon the scene, and wherever she looks there start up round her characters of extreme individuality and intensity who are branded for ever with the features she discerns in them. There are novelists, like Tolstoy and Jane Austen, who persuade us that their characters live and are complex by means of their effect upon many different people, who mirror them in the round. They move hither and thither whether their creator watches them or not. But we cannot imagine Rochester when he is apart from Jane Eyre, or rather we can only see him in different situations as she would have seen him in them, and to be always in love and always a governess is to go through the world with blinkers on one's eyes.

These are serious limitations, perhaps, and it may be true that they give her work a look of crudeness and violence beside that of more impersonal and more experienced artists. At the same time it is by reason of this marvellous gift of vision that she takes her place with the greatest novelists we have. No writer, that is to say, surpasses her in the power of making what she describes immediately visible to us. She seems to sit down to write from compulsion. The scenes in her mind are painted so boldly and in such strong colours that her hand (so we feel) drives rapidly across the paper, and trembles with the intensity of her thought. It is not surprising to hear that she did not enjoy writing her books, and yet that writing was the only occupation that could lift her up when the burden of sorrow and shame which life laid on her, weighted her to the ground. Every one of her books seems to be a superb gesture of defiance, bidding her torturers depart and leave her Queen of a splendid island of imagination. Like some hard-pressed captain, she summoned her powers together and proudly annihilated the enemy.

But although much has been said of her habit of describing actual people, and introducing scenes which had happened to her, the vividness of the result is not so easy to analyse. She had both an abnormal sensibility which made every figure and incident strike its pattern upon her mind, and also an extraordinary tenacity and toughness of purpose which drove her to test and investigate these impressions to the last ounce of them. 'I could never', she writes, 'rest in communication with strong discreet and refined minds, whether male or female, till I had passed the outworks of conventional reserve and crossed the threshold of confidence, and won a place by their hearts' very hearthstone.' It is by the 'heart's very hearthstone' that she begins her writing, with the light of it glowing on her page. Indeed, her production, whatever its faults, always seems to issue from a deep place where the fire is eternal. The peculiar virtues of her style, its character, its speed, its colour and strength, seem all of her own forging and to owe nothing to literary instruction or to the reading of many books. The smoothness of the professional writer, his ability to stuff out and sway his language as he chooses, was never learnt by her. She remains always unsophisticated, but with a power through sheer force of meaning of creating the word she needs and winging her way with a rhythm of her own. This mastery over language grew as she gained maturity as an artist; and in *Villette*, the last and greatest of her works, she is mistress not only of a strong and individual style, but of a style that is both variable and splendid. We are made to remember, too, her long toil with brush and pencil, for she has a strange gift, rare in a writer, of rendering the quality of colour and of texture in words, and thus investing many of her scenes with a curious brilliance and solidity.

> Yet it was merely a very pretty drawing room, and within it a boudoir, both spread with white carpets, on which seemed laid brilliant garlands of flowers; both ceiled with snowy moulding of white grapes and vine leaves, beneath which glowed in rich contrast crimson couches and ottomans; while the ornaments on the pale Parian mantelpiece were of sparkling Bohemia glass, ruby red; and between the windows large mirrors repeated the general blending of snow and fire.

We not only see that, we can almost touch it. She never heaps her colours, but lays a blue or a purple or her favourite crimson so rightly on the page that they paint the sentence as with actual pigment. Naturally, therefore, we should expect to find her a great landscape painter, a great lover of the air and the sky and all the pageant that lies between earth and heaven; nor may a student of hers tell whether he cares more for her people or for the keen air and the scent of the moor and the 'plumes of the storm' which surround them with such light and atmosphere, and such overwhelming poetry. Her descriptions, too, are not separate visions, as they tend to be so often with writers of less powerful gift, but work themselves into the heart of the book.

> It was a mile from Thornfield, in a lane noted for wild roses in summer, for nuts and blackberries in autumn, and even now possessing a few coral treasures in hips and haws, but whose best winter delight lay in its utter solitude and leafless repose. If a breath of air stirred, it made no sound here; for there was not a holly, not an evergreen to rustle, and the stripped hawthorn and hazel bushes were as still as the white worn stones which causewayed the middle of the path. Far and wide on each side there were only fields where no cattle now browsed, and the little brown birds which stirred occasionally looked like single russet leaves that had forgotten to drop.

How beautifully that spreads the mood of the moment over the face of the land!

But these are the details of a great literary gift. We go back to her books and sometimes this quality strikes us and sometimes that. But all the while we are conscious of something that is greater than one gift or another and is perhaps the quality that attaches us to books as to people – the quality, that is, of the writer's mind and personality. With their limitations and their great beauty these are stamped upon every page that Charlotte Brontë wrote. We do not need to know her story, or to have climbed the steep hill and gazed upon the stone house among the graves to feel her tremendous honesty and courage, and to know that she loved liberty and independence and the splendour of wild country, and men and women who are above all things passionate and true-minded. These are part of her as her imagination and genius are part of her; and they add to our admiration of her as a writer some peculiar warmth of feeling which makes us desire, when there is any question of doing her honour, to rise and salute her not only as a writer of genius, but as a very noble human being.

Hours in a Library

Let us begin by clearing up the old confusion between the man who loves learning and the man who loves reading, and point out that there is no connexion whatever between the two. A learned man is a sedentary, concentrated, solitary enthusiast, who searches through books to discover some particular grain of truth upon which he has set his heart. If the passion for reading conquers him, his gains dwindle and vanish between his fingers. A reader, on the other hand, must check the desire for learning at the outset; if knowledge sticks to him well and good, but to go in pursuit of it, to read on a system, to become a specialist or an authority, is very apt to kill what it suits us to consider the more humane passion for pure and disinterested reading.

In spite of all this, we can easily conjure up a picture which does service for the bookish man and raises a smile at his expense. We conceive a pale, attenuated figure in a dressing gown, lost in speculation, unable to lift a kettle from the hob, or address a lady without blushing, ignorant of the daily news, though versed in the catalogues of the secondhand booksellers, in whose dark premises he spends the hours of sunlight – a delightful character, no doubt, in his crabbed simplicity, but not in the least resembling that other to whom we would direct attention. For the true reader is essentially young. He is a man of intense curiosity; of ideas; open minded and communicative, to whom reading is more of the nature of brisk exercise in the open air than of sheltered study; he trudges the high road, he climbs higher and higher upon the hills until the atmosphere is almost too fine to breathe in; to him it is not a sedentary pursuit at all.

But, apart from general statements, it would not be hard to prove by an assembly of facts that the great season for reading is the season between the ages of eighteen and twenty-four. The bare list of what is read then fills the heart of older people with despair. It is not only that we read so many books, but that we had such books to read. If we wish to refresh our memories, let us take down one of those old notebooks which we have all, at one time or another, had a passion for beginning. Most of the pages are blank, it is true; but at the beginning we shall find a certain number very beautifully covered with a strikingly legible handwriting. Here we have written down the names of great writers in their order of merit; here we have copied out fine passages from the classics; here are lists of books to be read; and here, most interesting of all, lists of books that have actually been read, as the reader testifies with some youthful vanity by a dash of red ink. We will quote a list of the books that some one read in a past January at the age of twenty, most of them probably for the first time. 1. *Rhoda Fleming*. 2. *The Shaving of Shagpat*. 3. *Tom Jones*. 4. *The Laodicean*. 5. Dewey's *Psychology*. 6. The Book of Job. 7. Webbe's *Discourse of Poesie*. 8. *The Duchess of Malfi*. 9. *The Revenger's Tragedy*. And so he goes on from month to month, until, as such lists will, it suddenly stops in the month of June. But if we follow the reader through his months it is clear that he can have done practically nothing but read. Elizabethan literature is gone through with some thoroughness; he reads a great deal of Webster, Browning, Shelley, Spenser, and Congreve; Peacock he read from start to finish; and most of Jane Austen's novels two or three times over. He read the whole of Meredith, the whole of Ibsen, and a little of Bernard Shaw. We may be fairly certain, too, that the time not spent in reading was spent in some stupendous argument in which the Greeks were pitted against the modern, romance against realism, Racine against Shakespeare, until the lights were seen to have grown pale in the dawn.

The old lists are there to make us smile and perhaps sigh a little, but we would give much to recall also the mood in which this orgy of reading was done. Happily, this reader was no prodigy, and with a little thought we can most of us recall the stages at least of our own initiation. The books we read in childhood, having purloined them from some shelf supposed to be inaccessible, have something of the unreality and awfulness of a stolen sight of the dawn coming over quiet fields where the household is asleep. Peeping between the curtains we see strange shapes of misty trees which we hardly recognize, though we may remember them all our lives; for children have a strange premonition of what is to come. But the later reading of which the above list is an example is quite a different matter. For the first time, perhaps, all restrictions have been removed, we can read what we like; libraries are at our command, and, best of all, friends who find themselves in the same position. For days upon end we do nothing but read. It is a time of extraordinary excitement and exaltation. We seem to rush about recognizing heroes. There is a sort of wonderment in our minds that we ourselves are really doing this, and mixed with it an absurd arrogance and desire to show our familiarity with the greatest human beings who have ever lived in the world. The passion for knowledge is then at its keenest, or at least most confident, and we have, too, an intense singleness of mind which the great writers gratify by making it appear that they are at one with us in their estimate of what is good in life. And as it is necessary to hold one's own against someone who has adopted Pope, let us say, instead of Sir Thomas Browne, for a hero, we conceive a deep affection for these men, and feel that we know them not as other people know them, but privately by ourselves. We are fighting under their leadership, and almost in the light of their eyes. So we haunt the old bookshops and drag home folios and quartos, Euripides in wooden boards, and Voltaire in eighty-nine volumes octavo.

But those lists are curious documents, in that they seem to include scarcely any of the contemporary writers. Meredith and Hardy and Henry James were of course alive when this reader came to them, but they were already accepted among the classics. There is no man of his own generation who influences him as Carlyle, or Tennyson, or Ruskin influenced the young of their day. And this we believe to be very characteristic of youth, for unless there is some admitted giant he will have nothing to do with the smaller men, although they deal with the world he lives in. He will rather go back to the classics, and consort entirely with minds of the very first order. For the time being he holds himself aloof from all the activities of men, and, looking at them from a distance, judges them with superb severity.

Indeed, one of the signs of passing youth is the birth of a sense of fellowship with other human beings as we take our place among them. We should like to think that we keep our standard as high as ever; but we certainly take more interest in the writings of our contemporaries and pardon their lack of inspiration for the sake of something that brings them nearer to us. It is even arguable that we get actually more from the living, although they may be much inferior, than from the dead. In the first place there can be no secret vanity in reading our contemporaries, and the kind of admiration which they inspire is extremely warm and genuine, because in order to give way to our belief in them we have often to sacrifice some very respectable prejudice which does us credit. We have also to find our own reasons for what we like and dislike, which acts as a spur to our attention, and is the best way of proving that we have read the classics with understanding.

Thus to stand in a great bookshop crammed with books so new that their pages almost stick together, and the gilt on their backs is still fresh, has an excitement no less delightful than the old excitement of the secondhand bookstall. It is not perhaps so exalted. But the old hunger to know what the immortals thought has given place to a far more tolerant curiosity to know what our own generation is thinking. What do living men and women feel, what are their houses like and what clothes do they wear, what money have they and what food do they eat, what do they love and hate, what do they see of the surrounding world, and what is the dream that fills the spaces of their active lives? They tell us all these things in their books. In them we can see as much both of the mind and of the body of our time as we have eyes for seeing.

When such a spirit of curiosity has fully taken hold of us, the dust will soon lie thick upon the classics unless some necessity forces us to read them. For the living voices are, after all, the ones we understand the best. We can treat them as we treat our equals; they are guessing our riddles, and, what is perhaps more important, we understand their jokes. And we soon develop another taste, unsatisfied by the great – not a valuable taste, perhaps, but certainly a very pleasant possession – the taste for bad books. Without committing the indiscretion of naming names we know which authors can be trusted to produce yearly (for happily they are prolific) a novel, a book of poems or essays, which affords us indescribable pleasure. We owe a great deal to bad books; indeed, we come to count their authors and their heroes among those figures who play so large a part in our silent life. Something of the same sort happens in the case of the memoir writers and autobiographers, who have created almost a fresh branch of literature in our age. They are not all of them important people, but strangely enough, only the most important, the dukes and the statesmen, are ever really dull. The men and women who set out, with no excuse except perhaps that they saw the Duke of Wellington once, to confide to us their opinions, their quarrels, their aspirations and their diseases, generally end by becoming, for the time at least, actors in those private dramas with which we beguile our solitary walks and our sleepless hours. Refine all this out of our consciousness and we should be poor indeed. And then there are the books of facts and history, books about bees and wasps and industries and gold mines and Empresses and diplomatic intrigues, about rivers and savages, Trade Unions, and Acts of Parliament, which we always read and always, alas! forget. Perhaps we are not making out a good case for a bookshop when we have to confess that it gratifies so many desires which have apparently nothing to do with literature. But let us remember that here we have a literature in the making. From these new books our children will select the one or two by which we shall be known for ever. Here, if we could recognize it, lies some poem, or novel, or history which will stand up and speak with other ages about our age when we lie prone and silent as the crowd of Shakespeare's day is silent and lives for us only in the pages of his poetry.

This we believe to be true; and yet it is oddly difficult in the case of new books to know which are the real books and what it is that they are telling us, and which are the stuffed books which will come to pieces when they have lain about for a year or two. We can see that there are many books, and we are frequently told that everyone can write nowadays. That may be true; yet we do not doubt that at the heart of this immense volubility, this flood and foam of language, this irreticence and vulgarity and triviality, there lies the heat of some great passion which only needs the accident of a brain more happily turned than the rest to issue in a shape which will last from age to age. It should be our delight to watch this turmoil, to do battle with the ideas and visions of our own time, to seize what we can use, to kill what we consider worthless, and above all to realize that we must be generous to the people who are giving shape as best they can to the ideas within them. No age of literature is so little submissive to authority as ours, so free from the dominion of the great; none seems so wayward with its gifts of reverence, or so volatile in its experiments. It may well seem, even to the attentive, that there is no trace of school or aim in the work of our poets and novelists. But the pessimist is inevitable, and he shall not persuade us that our literature is dead, or prevent us from feeling how true and vivid a beauty flashes out as the young writers draw together to form their new vision, the ancient words of the most beautiful of living languages. Whatever we may have learnt from reading the classics we need now in order to judge the work of our contemporaries, for whenever there is life in them they will be casting their net out over some unknown abyss to snare new shapes, and we must throw our imaginations after them if we are to accept with understanding the strange gifts they bring back to us.

But if we need all our knowledge of the old writers in order to follow what the new writers are attempting, it is certainly true that we come from adventuring among new books with a far keener eye for the old. It seems that we should now be able to surprise their secrets; to look deep down into their work and see the parts come together, because we have watched the making of new books, and with eyes clear of prejudice can judge more truly what it is that they are doing, and what is good and what bad. We shall find, probably, that some of the great are less vulnerable than we thought them. Indeed, they are not so accomplished or so profound as some of our own time. But if in one or two cases this seems to be true, a kind of humiliation mixed with joy overcomes us in front of others. Take Shakespeare, or Milton, or Sir Thomas Browne. Our little knowledge of how things are done does not avail us much here, but it does lend an added zest to our enjoyment. Did we ever in our youngest days feel such amazement at their achievement as that which fills us now that we have sifted myriads of words and gone along uncharted ways in search of new forms for our new sensations? New books may be more stimulating and in some ways more suggestive than the old, but they do not give us that absolute certainty of delight which breathes through us when we come again to *Comus*, or *Lycidas*, *Urn Burial*, or *Anthony and Cleopatra*. Far be it from us to hazard any theory as to the nature of art. It may be that we shall never know more about it than we know by nature, and our longer experience of it teaches us this only – that of all our pleasures those we got from the great artists are indisputably among the best; and more we may not know. But, advancing no theory, we shall find one or two qualities in such works as these which we can hardly expect to find in books made within the span of our lifetime. Age itself may have an alchemy of its own. But this is true: you can read them as often as you will without finding that they have yielded any virtue and left a meaningless husk of words; and there is a complete finality about them. No cloud of suggestions hangs about them teasing us with a multitude of irrelevant ideas. But all our faculties are summoned to the task, as in the great moments of our own experience; and some consecration descends upon us from their hands which we return to life, feeling it more keenly and understanding it more deeply than before.

George Eliot

To read George Eliot attentively is to become aware how little one knows about her. It is also to become aware of the credulity, not very creditable to one's insight, with which, half consciously and partly maliciously, one had accepted the late Victorian version of a deluded woman who held phantom sway over subjects even more deluded than herself. At what moment and by what means her spell was broken it is difficult to ascertain. Some people attribute it to the publication of her Life. Perhaps George Meredith with his phrase about 'the mercurial little showman' and the 'errant woman' on the dais gave point and poison to the arrows of thousands incapable of aiming them so accurately but delighted to let fly. She became one of the butts for youth to laugh at, the convenient symbol of a group of serious people who were all guilty of the same idolatry and could be dismissed with the same scorn. Lord Acton had said that she was greater than Dante. Herbert Spencer exempted her novels, as if they were not novels, when he banned all fiction from the London Library. She was the pride and paragon of her sex. Moreover her private record was not more alluring than her public. Asked to describe an afternoon at the Priory, the story-teller always intimated that the memory of those serious Sunday afternoons had come to tickle his sense of humour. He had been so much alarmed by the grave lady in her low chair; he had been so anxious to say the intelligent thing. Certainly, the talk had been very serious, as a note in the fine clear hand of the great novelist bore witness. It was dated on the Monday morning, and she accused herself of having spoken without due forethought of Marivaux when she meant another; but no doubt, she said, her listener had already supplied the correction. Still, the memory of talking about Marivaux to George Eliot on a Sunday afternoon was not a romantic memory. It had faded with the passage of the years. It had not become picturesque.

Indeed, one cannot escape the conviction that the long, heavy face with its expression of serious and sullen and almost equine power has stamped itself depressingly upon the minds of people who remember George Eliot so that it looks out upon them from her pages. Mr. Gosse has lately described her as he saw her driving through London in a victoria –

a large, thick-set Sybil, dreamy and immobile,
whose massive features, somewhat grim when
seen in profile, were incongruously bordered by a
hat, always in the height of Paris fashion, which in
those days commonly included an immense
ostrich feather.

Lady Ritchie, with equal skill, has left a more intimate
indoor portrait.

She sat by the fire in a beautiful black satin gown,
with a green shaded lamp on the table beside her,
where I saw German books lying and pamphlets
and ivory paper-cutters. She was very quiet and
noble, with two steady little eyes and a sweet
voice. As I looked I felt her to be a friend, not
exactly a personal friend, but a good and benevolent impulse.

A scrap of her talk is preserved. 'We ought to respect our
influence', she said. 'We know by our own experience
how very much others affect our lives, and we must
remember that we in turn must have the same effect
upon others.' Jealously treasured, committed to memory,
one can imagine recalling the scene, repeating the words,
thirty years later and suddenly, for the first time, bursting
into laughter.

In all these records one feels that the recorder, even when he was in the actual presence, kept his distance and kept his head, and never read the novels in later years with the light of a vivid, or puzzling, or beautiful personality dazzling in his eyes. In fiction, where so much of personality is revealed, the absence of charm is a great lack; and her critics, who have been, of course, mostly of the opposite sex, have resented, half consciously perhaps, her deficiency in a quality which is held to be supremely desirable in women. George Eliot was not charming; she was not strongly feminine; she had none of those eccentricities and inequalities of temper which give to so many artists the endearing simplicity of children. One feels that to most people, as to Lady Ritchie, she was 'not exactly a personal friend, but a good and benevolent impulse'. But if we consider these portraits more closely we shall find that they are all the portraits of an elderly celebrated woman, dressed in black satin, driving in her victoria, a woman who has been through her struggle and issued from it with a profound desire to be of use to others but with no wish for intimacy save with the little circle who had known her in the days of her youth. We know very little about the days of her youth; but we do know that the culture, the philosophy, the fame, and the influence were all built upon a very humble foundation – she was the grand-daughter of a carpenter.

The first volume of her life is a singularly depressing record. In it we see her raising herself with groans and struggles from the intolerable boredom of petty provincial society (her father had risen in the world and become more middle class, but less picturesque) to be the assistant editor of a highly intellectual London review, and the esteemed companion of Herbert Spencer. The stages are painful as she reveals them in the sad soliloquy in which Mr. Cross condemned her to tell the story of her life. Marked in early youth as one 'sure to get something up very soon in the way of a clothing club', she proceeded to raise funds for restoring a church by making a chart of ecclesiastical history; and that was followed by a loss of faith which so disturbed her father that he refused to live with her. Next came the struggle with the translation of Strauss, which, dismal and 'soul-stupefying' in itself, can scarcely have been made less so by the usual feminine tasks of ordering a household and nursing a dying father, and the distressing conviction, to one so dependent upon affection, that by becoming a blue-stocking she was forfeiting her brother's respect. 'I used to go about like an owl', she said, 'to the great disgust of my brother.' 'Poor thing', wrote a friend who saw her toiling through Strauss with a statue of the risen Christ in front of her, 'I do pity her sometimes with her pale sickly face and dreadful headaches, and anxiety, too, about her father.' Yet, though we cannot read the story without a strong desire that the stages of her pilgrimage might have been made, if not more easy, at least more beautiful, there is a dogged determination in her advance upon the citadel of culture which raises it above our pity. Her development was very slow and very awkward but had the irresistible impetus behind it of a deep-seated and noble ambition. Every obstacle at length was thrust from her path. She knew everyone. She read everything. Her astonishing intellectual vitality had triumphed. Youth was over, but youth had been full of suffering. Then, at the age of thirty-five, at the height of her powers, and in the fullness of her freedom, she made the decision which was of such profound moment to her and still matters even to us, and went to Weimar alone with George Henry Lewes.

The books which followed so soon after her union testify in the fullest manner to the great liberation which had come to her with personal happiness. In themselves they provide us with a plentiful feast. Yet at the threshold of her literary career one may find in some of the circumstances of her life influences that turned her mind to the past, to the country village, to the quiet and beauty and simplicity of childish memories and away from herself and the present. We understand how it was that her first book was *Scenes of Clerical Life*, and not *Middlemarch*. Her union with Lewes had surrounded her with affection, but in view of the circumstances and of the conventions it had also isolated her. 'I wish it to be understood', she wrote in 1857, 'that I should never invite anyone to come and see me who did not ask for the invitation.' She had been 'cut off from what is called the world', she said later, but she did not regret it. By becoming thus marked, first by circumstances and later, inevitably, by her fame, she lost the power to move on equal terms unnoted among her kind; and the loss for a novelist was serious. Still, basking in the light and sunshine of *Scenes of Clerical Life*, feeling the large mature mind spreading itself with a luxurious sense of freedom in the world of her 'remotest past', to speak of loss seems inappropriate. Everything to such a mind was gain. All experience filtered down through layer after layer of perception and reflection enriching and nourishing. The utmost we can say, in qualifying her attitude towards fiction by what little we know of her life, is that she had taken to heart certain lessons not usually learnt early, if learnt at all, among which perhaps the most branded upon her was the melancholy virtue of tolerance; her sympathies are with the everyday lot, and play most happily in dwelling upon the homespun of ordinary joys and sorrows. She has none of that romantic intensity which is connected with a sense of one's own individuality, unsated and unsubdued, cutting its shape sharply upon the background of the world. What were the loves and sorrows of a snuffy old clergyman, dreaming over his whisky, to the fiery egotism of Jane Eyre?

The beauty of those first books, *Scenes of Clerical Life*, *Adam Bede*, *The Mill on the Floss*, is very great. It is impossible to estimate the merit of the Poysers, the Dodsons, the Gilfils, the Bartons, and the rest with all their surroundings and dependencies, because they have put on flesh and blood and we move among them, now bored, now sympathetic, but always with that unquestioning acceptance of all that they say and do which we accord to the great originals only. The flood of memory and humour which she pours so spontaneously into one figure, one scene after another, until the whole fabric of ancient rural England is revived, has so much in common with a natural process that it leaves us with little consciousness that there is anything to criticize. We accept; we expand; we feel the delicious warmth and release of spirit which the great creative writers alone procure for us. As one comes back to the books after years of absence they pour out, even against our expectation, the same store of energy and heat, so that we want more than anything to idle in the warmth as in the sun beating down from the red orchard wall. If there is an element of unthinking abandonment in thus submitting to the humours of Midland farmers and their wives, that, too, is right in the circumstances. We scarcely wish to analyse what we feel to be so largely and deeply human. And when we consider how distant the world of Shepperton and Hayslope is, and how remote the minds of farmers and agricultural labourers from those of most of George Eliot's readers, we can only attribute the ease and pleasure with which we ramble from farm house to smithy, from cottage parlour to rectory garden, to the fact that George Eliot makes us share their lives not in a spirit of condescension or of curiosity but in a spirit of sympathy. She is no satirist. The movement of her mind was too slow and cumbersome to lend itself to comedy. But she gathers in her large grasp a great bunch of the main elements of human nature and groups them loosely together with a tolerant and wholesome understanding which, as one finds upon re-reading, has not only kept her figures fresh and free but has given them an unexpected hold upon our laughter and tears. There is the famous Mrs. Poyser. It would have been easy to work her idiosyncrasies to death, and, as it is, perhaps George Eliot gets her laugh in the same place a little too often. But memory, after the book is shut, brings out, as sometimes in real life, the details and subtleties which some more salient characteristic has prevented us from noticing at the time. We recollect that her health was not good. There were occasions upon which she said nothing at all. She was patience itself with a sick child. She doted upon Totty. Thus one can muse and speculate about the greater number of George Eliot's characters, and find, even in the least important, a roominess and margin where those qualities lurk which she has no call to bring from their obscurity.

But in the midst of all this tolerance and sympathy, there are, even in the early books, moments of greater stress. Her humour has shown itself broad enough to cover a wide range of fools and failures, mothers and children, dogs and flourishing midland fields, farmers, sagacious or fuddled over their ale, horsedealers, inn-keepers, curates, and carpenters. Over them all broods a certain romance, the only romance that George Eliot allowed herself – the romance of the past. The books are astonishingly readable and have no trace of pomposity or pretence. But to the reader who holds a large stretch of her early work in view it will become obvious that the mist of recollection gradually withdraws. It is not that her power diminishes, for, to our thinking, it is at its highest in the mature *Middlemarch*. But the world of fields and farms no longer contents her. In real life she had sought her fortunes elsewhere; and though to look back into the past was calming and consoling, there are, even in the early works, traces of that troubled spirit, that exacting and questioning and baffled presence who was George Eliot herself. In *Adam Bede* there is a hint of her in Dinah. She shows herself far more openly and completely in Maggie in *The Mill on the Floss*. She is Janet in 'Janet's Repentance' and Romola, and Dorothea seeking wisdom and finding one scarcely knows what in marriage with Ladislaw. Those who fall foul of George Eliot do so, we incline to think, on account of her heroines: and with good reason; for there is no doubt that they bring out the worst of her, lead her into difficult places, make her self-conscious, didactic and occasionally vulgar. Yet if you could delete the whole sisterhood you would leave a much smaller and a much inferior world, albeit a world of greater artistic perfection and far superior jollity and comfort. In accounting for her failure, in so far as it was a failure, one recollects that she never wrote a story until she was thirty-seven, and that by the time she was thirty-seven she had come to think of herself with a mixture of pain and something like resentment. For long she preferred not to think of herself at all. Then, when the first flush of creative energy was exhausted and self-confidence had come to her, she wrote more and more from the personal standpoint, but she did so without the unhesitating abandonment of the young. Her self-consciousness is always marked when her heroines say what she herself would have said. She disguised them in every possible way. She granted them beauty and wealth into the bargain; she invented, more improbably, a taste for brandy. But the disconcerting and stimulating fact remained that she was compelled by the very power of her genius to step forth in person upon the quiet bucolic scene.

The noble and beautiful girl who insisted upon being born into the Mill on the Floss is the most obvious example of the ruin which a heroine can strew about her.

Humour controls her and keeps her lovable so long as she is small and can be satisfied by eloping with the gipsies or hammering nails into her doll; but she develops; and before George Eliot knows what has happened she has a full-grown woman on her hands demanding what neither gipsies nor dolls, nor St. Ogg's itself is capable of giving her. First Philip Wakem is produced and later Stephen Guest. The weakness of the one and the coarseness of the other have often been pointed out; but both, in their weakness and coarseness, illustrate not so much George Eliot's inability to draw the portrait of a man, as the uncertainty, the infirmity, and the fumbling which shook her hand when she had to conceive a fit mate for a heroine. She is in the first place driven beyond the home world she knew and loved, and forced to set foot in middle-class drawing rooms where young men sing all the summer morning and young women sit embroidering smoking caps for bazaars. She feels herself out of her element, as her clumsy satire of what she calls 'good society' proves.

Good society has its claret and its velvet carpets, its dinner engagements six weeks deep, its opera and its faëry ball rooms ... gets its science done by Faraday and its religion by the superior clergy who are to be met in the best houses; how should it have need of belief and emphasis?

There is no trace of humour or insight there, but only the vindictiveness of a grudge which we feel to be personal in its origin. But terrible as the complexity of our social system is in its demands upon the sympathy and discernment of a novelist straying across the boundaries, Maggie Tulliver did worse than drag George Eliot from her natural surroundings. She insisted upon the introduction of the great emotional scene. She must love; she must despair; she must be drowned clasping her brother in her arms. The more one examines the great emotional scenes the more nervously one anticipates the brewing and gathering and thickening of the cloud which will burst upon our heads at the moment of crisis in a shower of disillusionment and verbosity. It is partly that her hold upon dialogue, when it is not dialect, is slack; and partly that she seems to shrink with an elderly dread of fatigue from the effort of emotional concentration. She allows her heroines to talk too much. She has little verbal felicity. She lacks the unerring taste which chooses one sentence and compresses the heart of the scene within that. 'Whom are you going to dance with?' asked Mr. Knightley at the Westons' ball. 'With you, if you will ask me', said Emma; and she had said enough. Mrs. Casaubon would have talked for an hour and we should have looked out of the window.

Yet, dismiss the heroines without sympathy, confine George Eliot to the agricultural world of her 'remotest past', and you not only diminish her greatness but lose her true flavour. That greatness is hers we can have no doubt. The width of the prospect, the large strong outlines of the principal features, the ruddy light of the early books, the searching power and reflective richness of the later, tempt us to linger and expatiate beyond our limits. But it is upon the heroines that we would cast a final glance. 'I have always been finding out my religion since I was a little girl', says Dorothea Casaubon. 'I used to pray so much – now I hardly ever pray. I try not to have desires merely for myself ...' She is speaking for them all. That is their problem. They cannot live without religion, and they start out on the search for one when they are little girls. Each has the deep feminine passion for goodness, which makes the place where she stands, in aspiration and agony, the heart of the book – still and cloistered like a place of worship, but that she no longer knows to whom to pray. In learning they seek their goal; in the ordinary tasks of womanhood; in the wider service of their kind. They do not find what they seek, and we cannot wonder. The ancient consciousness of woman, charged with suffering and sensibility, and for so many ages dumb, seems in them to have brimmed and over-flowed and uttered a demand for something – they scarcely know what – for something that is perhaps incompatible with the facts of human existence. George Eliot had far too strong an intelligence to tamper with those facts, or to mitigate the truth because it was a stern one. Save for the supreme courage of their endeavour, the struggle ends, for her heroines, in tragedy, or in a compromise that is even more melancholy.

But their story is the incomplete version of the story of George Eliot herself. For her, too, the burden and the complexity of womanhood were not enough; she must reach beyond the sanctuary and pluck for herself the strange bright fruits of art and knowledge. Clasping them, as few women have ever clasped them, she would not renounce her own inheritance – the difference of view, the difference of standard – nor accept an inappropriate reward. Thus we behold her, a memorable figure, inordinately praised and shrinking from her fame, despondent, reserved, shuddering back into the arms of love as if there alone were satisfaction and, it might be, justification; at the same time reaching out with 'a fastidious yet hungry ambition' for all that life could offer the free and inquiring mind and confronting her feminine aspirations with the real world of men. Triumphant was the issue for her, whatever it may have been for her creations; and as we recollect all that she dared and achieved, how, crushed by sorrow, she mastered even that desolation and sought more knowledge and more understanding till the body, weighted with its double burden, sank and died worn out, we must lay upon her grave whatever we have it in our power to bestow of laurel and rose.

The Letters of Henry James

Who, on stepping from the cathedral dusk, the growl and boom of the organ still in the ears, and the eyes still shaded to observe better whatever intricacy of carving or richness of marble may there be concealed, can breast the stir of the street and instantly and briskly sum up and deliver his impressions? How discriminate, how formulate? How, Henry James may be heard grimly asking, dare you pronounce any opinion whatever upon me? In the first place only by taking cover under some such figure as implies that, still dazed and well-nigh drowned, our gesture at the finish is more one of exclamation than of interpretation. To soothe and to inspirit there comes, a moment later, the consciousness that, although in the eyes of Henry James our attempt is foredoomed to failure, nevertheless his blessing is upon it. Renewal of life, on such terms as we can grant it, upon lips, in minds, here in London, here among English men and women, would receive from him the most generous acknowledgment; and with a royal complacency, he would admit that our activities could hardly be better employed. Nor are we left to grope without a guide. It would not be easy to find a difficult task better fulfilled than by Mr. Percy Lubbock in his introduction and connecting paragraphs. It seems to us, and this not only before reading the letters but more emphatically afterwards, that the lines of inter-pretation he lays down are the true ones. They end – as he is the first to declare – in the heart of darkness; but any understanding that we may have won of a difficult problem is at every point fortified and corrected by the help of his singularly thoughtful and intimate essay. His intervention is always illuminating.

It must be admitted that these remarks scarcely seem called for by anything specially abstruse in the first few chapters. If ever a young American proved himself capa-ble of giving a clear and composed account of his experi-ences in Europe during the seventies of the last century that young American was Henry James. He recounts his seeings and doings, his dinings out and meetings, his country house visits, like a guest too well-bred to show surprise even if he feels it. A 'cosmopolitanized American', as he calls himself, was far more likely, it appears, to find things flat than to find them surprising; to sink into the depths of English civilization as if it were a soft feather bed inducing sleep and warmth and secu-rity rather than shocks and sensations. Henry James, of course, was much too busy recording impressions to fall asleep; it only appears that he never did anything, and never met anyone, in those early days, capable of rousing him beyond the gay and sprightly mood so easily and amusingly sustained in his letters home. Yet he went everywhere; he met everyone, as the sprinkling of famous names and great occasions abundantly testifies. Let one fair specimen suffice:

Yesterday I dined with Lord Houghton – with Gladstone, Tennyson, Dr. Schliemann (the excavator of old Mycenae, &c.), and half a dozen other men of 'high culture'. I sat next but one to the Bard and heard most of his talk, which was all about port wine and tobacco; he seems to know much about them, and can drink a whole bottle of port at a sitting with no incommodity. He is very swarthy and scraggy, and strikes one at first as much less handsome than his photos: but gradually you see that it's a face of genius. He had I know not what simplicity, speaks with a strange rustic accent and seemed altogether like a creature of some primordial English stock, a thousand miles away from American manufacture. Behold me after dinner conversing affably with Mr. Gladstone – not by my own seeking, but by the almost importunate affection of Lord H. But I was glad of a chance to feel the 'personality' of a great political leader – or as G. is now thought here even, I think, by his partisans, ex-leader. That of Gladstone is very fascinating – his urbanity extreme – his eye that of a man of genius – and his apparent self-surrender to what he is talking of without a flaw. He made a great impression on me – greater than anyone I have seen here: though 'tis perhaps owing to my naïveté, and unfamiliarity with statesmen ...

And so to the Oxford and Cambridge boat-race. The impression is well and brightly conveyed; what we miss, perhaps, is any body of resistance to the impression – any warrant for thinking that the receiving mind is other than a stretched white sheet. The best comment upon that comes in his own words a few pages later. 'It is something to have learned how to write.' If we look upon many of these early pages as experiments in the art of writing by one whose standard of taste exacts that small things must be done perfectly before big things are even attempted, we shall understand that their perfection is of the inexpressive kind that often precedes a late maturity. He is saying all that his means allow him to say. Moreover, he is saying it already, as most good letter writers learn to say it, not to an individual but to a chosen assembly. 'It is, indeed, I think, the very essence of a good letter to be shown', he wrote; 'it is wasted if it is kept for one ... I give you full leave to read mine aloud at your soirees!' Therefore, if we refrain from quotation, it is not that passages of the necessary quality are lacking. It is, rather, that while he writes charmingly, intelligently and adequately of this, that and the other, we begin by guessing and end by resenting the fact that his mind is elsewhere. It is not the dinner parties – a hundred and seven in one season – nor the ladies and gentlemen, nor even the Tennysons and the Gladstones that interest him primarily; the pageant passes before him: the impressions ceaselessly descend; and yet as we watch we also wait for the clue, the secret of it all. It is, indeed, clear that if he discharged the duties of his position with every appearance of equanimity the choice of the position itself was one of momentous importance, constantly requiring examination, and, with its promise of different possibilities, harassing his peace till the end of time. On what spot of the civilized globe was he to settle? His vibrations and vacillations in front of that problem suffer much in our report of them, but in the early days the case against America was simply that '... it takes an old civilization to set a novelist in motion'.

Next, Italy presented herself; but the seductions of 'the golden climate' were fatal to work. Paris had obvious advantages, but the drawbacks were equally positive – 'I have seen almost nothing of the literary fraternity, and there are fifty reasons why I should not become intimate with them. I don't like their wares, and they don't like any others; and, besides, they are not *accueillants*'. London exercised a continuous double pressure of attraction and repulsion to which finally he succumbed, to the extent of making his headquarters in the metropolis without shutting his eyes to her faults. 'I am attracted to London in spite of the long list of reasons why I should not be; I think it, on the whole, the best point of view in the world ... But the question is interminable.' When he wrote that, he was thirty-seven; a mature age; an age at which the native growing confidently in his own soil is already putting forth whatever flower fate ordains and natural conditions allow. But Henry James had neither roots nor soil; he was of the tribe of wanderers and aliens; a winged visitant, ceaselessly circling and seeking, unattached, uncommitted, ranging hither and thither at his own free will, and only at length precariously settling and delicately inserting his proboscis in the thickset lusty blossoms of the old garden beds.

Here, then, we distinguish one of the strains, always to some extent present in the letters before us, from which they draw their unlikeness to any others in the language, and, indeed, bring us at times to doubt whether they are 'in the language' at all. If London is primarily a point of view, if the whole field of human activity is only a prospect and a pageant, then we cannot help asking, as the store of impressions heaps itself up, what is the aim of

the spectator, what is the purpose of his hoard? A spectator, alert, aloof, endlessly interested, endlessly obser-
vant, Henry James undoubtedly was; but as obviously,
though not so simply, the long drawn process of adjustment and preparation was from first to last controlled
and manipulated by a purpose which, as the years went
by, only dealt more powerfully and completely with the
treasures of a more complex sensibility. Yet, when we
look to find the purpose expressed, to see the material in
the act of transmutation, we are met by silence, we are
blindly waved outside. 'To write a series of good little
tales I deem ample work for a life time. It's at least a relief
to have arranged one's life time.' The words are youthful,
perhaps intentionally light but few and frail as they are,
they have almost alone to bear the burden built upon
them, to answer the questions and quiet the suspicions
of those who insist that a writer must have a mission and
proclaim it aloud. Scarcely for a moment does Henry
James talk of his writing; never for an instant is the
thought of it absent from his mind. Thus, in the letters to
Stevenson abroad we hear behind everything else a
brooding murmur of amazement and horror at the notion
of living with savages. How, he seems to be asking himself,
while on the surface all is admiration and affection, can
he endure it – how could I write my books if I lived in
Samoa with savages? All refers to his writing; all points in
to that preoccupation. But so far as actual statement goes

the books might have sprung as silently and spontaneously as daffodils in spring. No notice is taken of their birth. Nor does it matter to him what people say. Their remarks are probably wide of the point, or if they have a passing truth they are uttered in unavoidable ignorance of the fact that each book is a step onward in a gradual process of evolution, the plan of which is onward only to the author himself. He remains inscrutable. silent, and assured.

How, then, are we to explain the apparent inconsistency of his disappointment when, some years later, the failure of *The Bostonians* and *Princess Casamassima* brought him face to face with the fact that he was not destined to be a popular novelist –

> ... I am still staggering [he wrote] a good deal under the mysterious and to me inexplicable injury wrought – apparently – upon my situation by my two last novels, the Bostonians and the Princess, from which I expected so much and derived so little. They have reduced the desire, and the demand, for my productions to zero – as I judge from the fact that though I have for a good while past been writing a number of good short things, I remain irremediably unpublished.

Compensations at once suggested themselves; he was 'really in better form than ever' and found himself 'holding the "critical world" at large in singular contempt' but we have Mr. Lubbock's authority for supposing that it was chiefly a desire to retrieve the failure of the novels that led him to strive so strenuously, and in the end so disastrously, for success upon the stage. Success and failure upon the lips of a man who never for a moment doubted the authenticity of his genius or for a second lowered his standard of the artist's duty have not their ordinary meaning. Perhaps we may hold that failure in the sense that Henry James used it meant, more than anything, failure on the part of the public to receive. That was the public's fault, but that did not lessen the catastrophe or make less desirable the vision of an order of things where the public gratefully and with understanding accepts at the artists' hands what is, after all, the finest essence, transmuted and returned, of the public itself. When *Guy Domville* failed, and Henry James for one 'abominable quarter of an hour' faced the 'yelling barbarians' and 'learned what could be the savagery of their disappointment that one wasn't perfectly the same as everything else they had ever seen' he had no doubt of his genius; but he went home to reflect:

I have felt for a long time past that I have fallen
upon evil days – every sign and symbol of one's
being in the least wanted, anywhere or by anyone,
having so utterly failed. A new generation, that I
know not, and mainly prize not, has taken universal possession.

The public henceforward appeared to him, so far as it
appeared at all, a barbarian crowd incapable of taking in
their rude paws the beauty and delicacy that he had to
offer. More and more was he confirmed in his conviction
that an artist can neither live with the public, write for it,
nor seek his material in the midst of it. A select group,
representative of civilization, had at the same time
protested its devotion, but how far can one write for a
select group? Is not genius itself restricted, or at least
influenced in its very essence, by the consciousness that
its gifts are to the few, its concern with the few, and its
revelation apparent only to scattered enthusiasts who
may be the advance guard of the future or only a little
band strayed from the high road and doomed to extinc-
tion while civilization marches irresistibly elsewhere? All
this Henry James poised, pondered, and held in debate.
No doubt the influence upon the direction of his work
was profound. But for all that he went serenely forward;
bought a house, bought a typewriter, shut himself up,
surrounded himself with furniture of the right period,

and was able at the critical moment by the timely, though rash, expenditure of a little capital to ensure that certain hideous new cottages did not deface his point of view. One admits to a momentary malice. The seclusion is so deliberate; the exclusion so complete. All within the sanctuary is so prosperous and smooth. No private responsibilities harassed him; no public duties claimed him; his health was excellent and his income, in spite of his protests to the contrary, more than adequate to his needs. The voice that issued from the hermitage might well speak calmly, subtly, of exquisite emotions, and yet now and then we are warned by something exacting and even acid in its tone that the effects of seclusion are not altogether benign. 'Yes. Ibsen is ugly, common, hard, prosaic, bottomlessly bourgeois ...' 'But, oh, yes, dear Louis, [*Tess of the D'Urbervilles*] is vile. The pretence of "sexuality" is only equalled by the absence of it, and the abomination of the language by the author's reputation for style.' The lack of 'aesthetic curiosity' in Meredith and his circle was highly to be deplored. The artist in him 'was nothing to the good citizen and liberalized bourgeois'. The works of Tolstoy and Dostoevsky are 'fluid puddings', and 'when you ask me if I don't feel Dostoevsky's "mad jumble, that flings things down in a heap" nearer truth and beauty than the picking up and composing that you instance in Stevenson, I reply with emphasis that I feel nothing of the sort'. It is true that in order to keep these points at their sharpest one has had to brush aside a mass of qualification and explanation which make each the apex of a formidable body of criticism. It is only for a moment that the seclusion seems cloistered, and the feelings of an artist confounded with those of a dilettante.

Yet as that second flits across the mind, with the chill of a shadow brushing the waves, we realize what a catastrophe for all of us it would have been if the prolonged experiment, the struggle and the solitude of Henry James's life had ended in failure. Excuses could have been found both for him and for us. It is impossible, one might have said, for the artist not to compromise, or, if he persists in his allegiance, then, almost inevitably, he must live apart, for ever alien, slowly perishing in his isolation. The history of literature is strewn with examples of both disasters. When, therefore, almost perceptibly at a given moment, late in the story, something yields, something is overcome, something dark and dense glows in splendour, it is as if the beacon flamed bright on the hilltop; as if before our eyes the crown of long deferred completion and culmination swung slowly into place. Not columns but pages, and not pages but chapters, might be filled with comment and attempted analysis of this late and mighty flowering, this vindication, this crowded gathering together and superb welding into shape of all the separate strands, alien instincts, irreconcilable desires of the twofold nature. For, as we dimly perceive, here at last two warring forces have coalesced; here, by a prodigious effort of concentration, the field of human activity is brought into fresh focus, revealing new horizons, new landmarks, and new lights upon it of right and wrong.

But it is for the reader at leisure to delve in the rich material of the later letters and build up from it the complex figure of the artist in his completeness. If we choose two passages – one upon conduct, the other upon the gift of a leather dressing case – to represent Henry James in his later mood we purposely brush aside a thousand others which have innumerable good claims to be put in their place.

> If there be a wisdom in not feeling – to the last throb – the great things that happen to us, it is a wisdom that I shall never either know or esteem. Let your soul live – it's the only life that isn't, on the whole, a sell ...

> That [the dressing case] is the grand fact of the situation – that is the tawny lion, portentous creature in my path. I can't get past him, I can't get round him, and on the other hand he stands glaring at me, refusing to give way and practically blocking all my future. I can't live with him, you

see; because I can't live *up* to him. His claims, his pretensions, his dimensions, his assumptions and consumptions, above all the manner in which he causes every surrounding object (on my poor premises or within my poor range) to tell a dingy, or deplorable tale – all this makes him the very scourge of my life, the very blot on my scutcheon. He doesn't regild that rusty metal – he simply takes up an attitude of gorgeous swagger, straight in front of all the rust and the rubbish, which makes me look as if I had stolen *somebody else's* (regarnished *blason*) and were trying to palm it off as my own ... *He is out of the picture* – out of *mine*; and behold me condemned to live for ever with that canvas turned to the wall. Do you know what that means?

And so on and so on. There, portentous and prodigious, we hear unmistakably the voice of Henry James. There, to our thinking, we have exploded in our ears the report of his enormous, sustained, increasing, and overwhelming love of life. It issues from whatever tortuous channels and dark tunnels like a flood at its fullest. There is nothing too little, too large, too remote, too queer for it not to flow round, float off and make its own. Nothing in the end has chilled or repressed him; everything has fed and filled him; the saturation is complete. The labours of the morning might be elaborate and austere. There remained an irrepressible fund of vitality which the flying hand at midnight addressed fully and affectionately to friend after friend, each sentence, from the whole fling of his person to the last snap of his fingers, firmly fashioned and throwing out at its swiftest well nigh incredible felicities of phrase.

The only difficulty, perhaps, was to find an envelope that would contain the bulky product, or any reason, when two sheets were blackened, for not filling a third. Truly, Lamb House was no sanctuary, but rather a 'small, crammed and wholly unlucrative hotel', and the hermit no meagre solitary but a tough and even stoical man of the world, English in his humour, Johnsonian in his sanity, who lived every second with insatiable gusto and in the flux and fury of his impressions obeyed his own injunction to remain 'as solid and fixed and dense as you can'. For to be as subtle as Henry James one must also be as robust; to enjoy his power of exquisite selection one must have 'lived and loved and cursed and floundered and enjoyed and suffered', and, with the appetite of a giant, have swallowed the whole.

Yet, if he shared with magnanimity, if he enjoyed hugely, there remained something incommunicable, something reserved, as if, in the last resort, it was not to us that he turned, nor from us that he received, nor into our hands that he placed his offerings. There they stand, the many books, products of 'an inexhaustible sensibility', all with the final seal upon them of artistic form, which, as it imposes its stamp, sets apart the object thus consecrated and makes it no longer part of ourselves. In this impersonality the maker himself desired to share – 'to take it', as he said, 'wholly, exclusively with the pen (the style, the genius) and absolutely not at all with the person', to be 'the mask without the face', the alien in our midst, the worker who when his work is done turns even from that and reserves his confidence for the solitary hour, like that at midnight when, alone on the threshold of creation, Henry James speaks aloud to himself 'and the prospect clears and flushes, and my poor blest old genius pats me so admirably and lovingly on the back that I turn, I screw round, and bend my lips to passionately, in my gratitude, kiss its hands'. So that is why, perhaps, as life swings and clangs, booms and reverberates, we have the sense of an altar of service, of sacrifice, to which, as we pass out, we bend the knee.

John Evelyn

Should you wish to make sure that your birthday will be celebrated three hundred years hence, your best course is, undoubtedly, to keep a diary. Yet most of us prefer to put our trust in poems, plays, novels, and histories. One in a generation, perhaps, has the courage to lock his genius in a private book and the humour to gloat over a fame which will be his only in the grave. There can be no doubt that the good diarists are those who write either for themselves or for a posterity so distant that it can safely hear every secret and justly weigh every motive. For such an audience there is no need either of affectation or of restraint. But a diary written to be published in the author's lifetime is no better than a private version of the newspaper, and often worse. The good opinion of our contemporaries means so much to us that it is well worth while to tell them lies.

But though these considerations may be just they are not on this occasion much to the point. Whatever else John Evelyn may have been he was neither introspective nor vindictive. The diary, for whose sake we are remembering his three-hundredth birthday, is sometimes composed like a memoir, sometimes jotted down like a calendar. But he never used its pages to reveal the secrets of his heart, and all he wrote might have been read aloud in the evening to his children. If we wonder, then, why we still trouble to read what we must consider the uninspired work of a good man, we have to confess what everybody knows – that it is impossible to read works of genius all day long. We have to confess that this reading, about which so many fine things have been said, is for the most part mere dreaming and idling; lying in a chair with a book; watching the butterflies on the dahlias; a profitless occupation which no critic has taken the trouble to investigate, and on whose behalf only the moralist can find a good word to say. For he will allow it to be an innocent employment, and happiness, though derived from trivial sources, has probably done more to prevent human beings from changing their religions and killing their kings than either philosophy or the pulpit.

It is indeed well, before reading much further in Evelyn's book, to decide where it is that our modern view of happiness differs from his. Undoubtedly ignorance is at the bottom of it. No one can read the story of Evelyn's foreign travels without envying in the first place his simplicity of mind, in the second his activity. To take a simple example of the difference between us. A butterfly will sit motionless on a flower while a wheelbarrow is trundled past it. But touch the tip of its wing with shadow and it is instantly up in the air. Presumably, then, a butterfly has either small sense of sound or none. Here, no doubt, we are much on a par with Evelyn. But as for going into the house to fetch a knife with which to dissect a Red Admiral's head, no sane person in the twentieth century would entertain such a notion for a second. Individually we may know as little as Evelyn, but collectively we know so much that there is little incentive to make private discoveries. We seek the encyclopaedia, not the scissors; and know in ten minutes not only more than was known to Evelyn in his lifetime, but that the mass of knowledge is so vast that it is scarcely worth while to possess a crumb. Ignorant, yet justly confident that with his own hands he might advance not merely his private knowledge but the knowledge of mankind, Evelyn dabbled in all the arts and sciences, ran about the Continent for ten years, gazed with unflagging gusto upon hairy women and elephants, magic stones and rational dogs, and drew inferences and framed speculations which are now only to be matched by listening to the talk of old women round the village pump. The moon, they say, is so much larger than usual this autumn that no mushrooms will grow and the carpenter's wife will be brought to bed of twins. So Evelyn, Fellow of the Royal Society, a gentleman of the highest culture and intelligence, carefully noted all comets and portents, and thought it a sinister omen when a whale came up the Thames. Once before this happened, in the year 1658. 'That year died Cromwell.' Nature certainly stimulated the devotion of her seventeenth-century admirers by displays of violence and eccentricity from which she now refrains. There were storms, floods, and droughts; the Thames frozen hard; comets flaring in the sky. If a cat so much as kittened in Evelyn's bed the kitten was inevitably gifted with eight legs, six ears, two bodies, and two tails.

But to return to happiness. It sometimes appears that if there is an insoluble difference between our ancestors and ourselves it is that we draw our happiness from different sources. We rate the same things at different values. Something of this we may ascribe to their ignorance and our knowledge. But are we to suppose that ignorance alters the nerves and the affections? Are we to believe that it would have been an intolerable penance for us to live familiarly with the Elizabethans? Should we have found it necessary to leave the room because of Shakespeare's habits, and to have refused Queen Elizabeth's invitation to dine? Perhaps so. For Evelyn was a sober man of unusual refinement, and yet he pressed into a torture chamber as we crowd to see the lions fed.

... they first bound his wrists with a strong rope or small cable, and one end of it to an iron ring made fast to the wall about four foot from the floor, and then his feet with another cable, fastened about five feet farther than his utmost length to another ring on the floor of the room. Thus suspended, and yet lying but aslant, they slid a horse of wood under the rope which bound his feet, which so exceedingly stiffened it, as severed the fellow's joints in miserable sort, drawing him out at length in an extraordinary manner, he having only a pair of linen drawers upon his naked body.

And so on. Evelyn watched this to the end, and then remarked that 'the spectacle was so uncomfortable that I was not able to stay the sight of another', as we might say that the lions growl so loud and the sight of raw meat is so unpleasant that we will now visit the penguins. Allowing for his discomfort, there is enough discrepancy between his view of pain and ours to make us wonder whether we see any fact with the same eyes, marry any woman from the same motives, or judge any conduct by the same standards. To sit passive when muscles tore and bones cracked, not to flinch when the wooden horse was raised higher and the executioner fetched a horn and poured two buckets of water down the man's throat, to suffer this iniquity on a suspicion of robbery which the man denied – all this seems to put Evelyn in one of those cages where we still mentally seclude the riff-raff of Whitechapel. Only it is obvious that we have somehow got it wrong. If we could maintain that our susceptibility to suffering and love of justice were proof that all our humane instincts were as highly developed as these, then we could say that the world improves, and we with it. But let us get on with the diary.

In 1652, when it seemed that things had settled down unhappily enough, 'all being entirely in the rebels' hands', Evelyn returned to England with his wife of twelve, his Tables of Veins and Arteries, his Venetian glass and the rest of his curiosities, to lead the life of a country gentleman of strong Royalist sympathies at Deptford. What with going to church and going to town, settling his accounts and planting his garden – 'I planted the orchard at Sayes Court; new moon, wind west.' – his time was spent much as ours is. But there was one difference which it is difficult to illustrate by a single quotation because the evidence is scattered all about in little insignificant phrases. The general effect of them is that he used his eyes. The visible world was always close to him. The visible world has receded so far from us that to hear all this talk of buildings and gardens, statues and carving, as if the look of things assailed one out of doors as well as in, and were not confined to a few small canvases hung upon the wall, seems strange. No doubt there are a thousand excuses for us; but hitherto we have been finding excuses for him. Wherever there was a picture to be seen by Julio Romano, Polydore, Guido, Raphael, or Tintoretto, a finely built house, a prospect, or a garden nobly designed, Evelyn stopped his coach to look at it, and opened his diary to record his opinion. On August 27 Evelyn, with Dr. Wren and others, was in St. Paul's surveying 'the general decay of that ancient and venerable church'; held with Dr. Wren another judgment from the rest; and had a mind to build it with 'a noble cupola, a form of church building not as yet known in England but of wonderful grace', in which Dr. Wren concurred. Six days later the Fire of London altered their plans. It was Evelyn again who, walking by himself, chanced to look in at the window of 'a poor solitary thatched house in a field in our parish', there saw a young man carving at a crucifix, was overcome with an enthusiasm which does him the utmost credit, and carried Grinling Gibbons and his carving to Court.

Indeed, it is all very well to be scrupulous about the sufferings of worms and sensitive to the dues of servant girls, but how pleasant also if, with shut eyes, one could call up street after street of beautiful houses. A flower is red; the apples rosy-gilt in the afternoon sun; a picture has charm, especially as it displays the character of a grandfather and dignifies a family descended from such a scowl; but these are scattered fragments – little relics of beauty in a world that has grown indescribably drab. To our charge of cruelty Evelyn might well reply by pointing to Bayswater and the purlieus of Clapham; and if he should assert that nothing now has character or conviction, that no farmer in England sleeps with an open coffin at his bedside to remind him of death, we could not retort effectually offhand. True, we like the country. Evelyn never looked at the sky.

But to return. After the Restoration Evelyn emerged in full possession of a variety of accomplishments which in our time of specialists seems remarkable enough. He was employed on public business; he was Secretary to the Royal Society; he wrote plays and poems; he was the first authority upon trees and gardens in England; he submitted a design for the rebuilding of London; he went into the question of smoke and its abatement – the lime trees in St. James's Park being, it is said, the result of his cogitations; he was commissioned to write a history of the Dutch war – in short, he completely outdid the Squire of 'The Princess', whom in many respects he anticipated –

> A lord of fat prize oxen and of sheep,
> A raiser of huge melons and of pine,
> A patron of some thirty charities,
> A pamphleteer on guano and on grain,
> A quarter sessions chairman abler none.

All that he was, and perhaps shared with Sir Walter another characteristic which Tennyson does not mention. He was, we cannot help suspecting, something of a bore. Or what is this quality, or absence of quality, which checks our sympathy? It is partly that he was better than his neighbours; partly that, though he deplored the vices of his age, he could never keep away from the centre of them. The 'luxurious dallying and profaneness' of the Court, the sight of 'Mrs. Nelly' looking over her garden wall and holding 'very familiar discourse' with King Charles on the green walk below, caused him acute disgust; but he could never make up his mind to break with the Court and retire to 'my poor, but quiet villa', which was, of course, one of the show places of England. Then, though he loved his daughter Mary, his grief at her death did not prevent him from counting the number of empty coaches drawn by six horses apiece that attended her funeral. His women friends combined virtue with beauty to such an extent that we can hardly credit them with wit into the bargain. Poor Mrs. Godolphin, at least, whom he celebrated in a sincere and touching biography, 'loved to be at funerals' and chose habitually the 'dryest and leanest morsels of meat', which may be the habits of an angel but do not present her friendship with Evelyn in an alluring light. The whole of our case against Evelyn, however, is summed up in the account of a visit which Pepys paid him on November 6, 1665. First Evelyn showed him some 'painting in little: then in distemper, in Indian ink, water-colour, graving and, above all, the whole secret of mezzo-tint and the manner of it'. He then read his discourse 'about gardenage, which will be a most pleasant piece'. Then a play or two of his making, 'very good, but not as he conceits them I think to be'; then he displayed his Hortus Hyemalis; and finally read aloud, 'though with too much gusto, some little poems of his own that were not transcendent ... among others, one of a lady looking in at a gate and being pecked at by an eagle that was there'. 'In line', Pepys concluded at the end of the long morning's entertainment, 'a most excellent person he is, and must be allowed a little for a little conceitedness; but he may well be so, being a man so much above others.'

Evelyn, as we are bound to remark after dipping into Pepys, was no genius. His writing is opaque rather than transparent. We see no depths through it, nor any very secret movements of mind and heart. He can neither make us hate a regicide nor love Mrs. Godolphin beyond reason. But even as we drowse, somehow or other the bygone gentleman sets up, through three centuries, a perceptible tingle of communication, so that without laying stress upon anything in particular we are taking notice all the time. His hypocritical modesty about his own garden is no less evident than his acidity about the gardens of others. The hens at Sayes Court, we may be sure, laid the best eggs in England. When the Tsar drove a wheelbarrow through his holly hedge his cry is that of a man in agony. Editors who wonder at the non-appearance of Mrs. Evelyn should reflect that she was chiefly occupied in dusting china and cleaning ink stains from the carpets. He was constantly asked to act as trustee; discharged his duties punctiliously, and yet grumbled at the waste of his time. Still he had a heart. Though a formal he was a very affectionate man. If paternal egotism probably hastened the death of the little prodigy Richard, he carried the memory of him throughout his life, and sighed deeply, not effusively – for the man with the long-drawn sensitive face was never effusive – when, 'after evening prayers was my child buried near the rest of his brothers – my very dear children'. He was not an artist, perhaps; yet as an artistic method this of going on with the day's story circumstantially, bringing in people who will never be mentioned again, leading up to crises which never take place, has an undoubted merit. On one page we are agog to hear that Evelyn has a mind to visit Sir Thomas Browne. The journey to Norwich in the flying chariot with six horses is precisely described, with the talk by the way. But when at length Evelyn meets Sir Thomas all he has to say of him is that he owns many curiosities; thinks Norfolk a good county for birds; and states that the people of Norwich have lost the art of squaring flints, which, of course, sets Evelyn off upon buildings and flower gardens and Sir Thomas Browne is never mentioned again.

Never to mention people again is a piece of advice that psychological novelists might well lay to heart. All through Evelyn's pages people are coming into the room and going out. The greater number we scarcely notice; the door shuts upon them and they disappear. But now and then the sight of a vanishing coat tail suggests more than a whole figure sitting still in a full light. Perhaps it is that we catch them unawares. Little they think that for three hundred years and more they will be looked at in the act of jumping a gate or observing, like the old Marquis of Argyle, that the turtle doves in the aviary are owls. There is a certain hot-tempered Captain Wray, for instance, upon whom we linger with unsatisfied affection. We are only told that he was choleric; that he had a dog who killed a goat; that he was for shooting the goat's owner; that when his horse fell down a precipice he was for shooting the horse; and, finally, that coming to Geneva, he 'fell so mightily in love with one of Monsieur Saladine's daughters that, with much persuasion, he could not be prevailed on to think on his journey into France, the season now coming on extremely hot', 'Yet', says Evelyn, 'the ladies of Geneva are not beautiful.' They have 'something full throats'. That is all there is about Captain Wray, but it is enough to start us upon speculations too numerous and too little authentic to be given here. And though the dusk has long closed upon Captain Wray and his bride – who, since the captain was choleric, the season hot, and the goitre prevalent, may never have become his bride after all – we are still curious, as is not usual at the end of psychological novels, to know what became of them. Mr. Maynard Smith, had he reached that point, might have told us. For his commentary upon the early life and education of John Evelyn is the very book that an idle reader, reading as much with his eye off the page as on, must rejoice in not only because so much of its information is necessary but because so much of it is superfluous. The reason why Evelyn's father refused a knighthood is illuminating; but it is difficult to see in what respect our knowledge of Evelyn's father's beard is improved by knowing that the Tudors wore beards, that Shakespeare mentioned them, and that the Puritans slept with theirs enclosed in cardboard boxes.

Indeed, had we to give an excuse for wasting our time first over Evelyn, then over Mr. Smith's commentary upon Evelyn, which promises and will, we hope, fulfil its promise of exceeding Evelyn himself in length, we could only vaguely and falteringly explain that, whether alive or dead, good or bad, human beings have a hold upon our sympathies. That Evelyn had his faults is true; that we could not have spent an hour in his company without grave disagreement is also probable – though to have been shown over Wotton by the master in his old age when his gardens were flourishing, his grandson doing him credit, his sorrows smoothed out, and the Latin quotations falling pat from his lips, would have been a thing to stick in the memory; but, faults and limitations notwithstanding, he lived for 84 years and kept a record of 55 of them. That is enough for us. For without saying in the old language that he has taught us a lesson or provided an example, we cannot deny that the spectacle of human life on such a scale is full of delight. First we have the oddity of it; then the difference; then as the years go by the sense of coming to know the man better and better. When that is established, the circle in which he moves becomes plain; we see his friends and their doings; so that by degrees it is not one person but a whole society of people whom we watch at their concerns. Fate shepherded them all very straitly. There was no getting out of death or age; nor, though Evelyn protested, could he escape burial in the stone chancel of a church instead of lying in earth with flowers growing over him. All this provokes thought – idle thought, it is true, but of the kind that fills the mind with Evelyn's presence and brings him back, in the sunshine, to walk among the trees.

On Re-reading Novels

So there are to be new editions of Jane Austen and the Brontës and George Meredith. Left in trains, forgotten in lodging-houses, thumbed and tattered to destruction, the old ones have served their day, and for the newcomers in their new houses there are to be new editions and new readings and new friends. It speaks very well for the Georgians. It is still more to the credit of the Victorians. In spite of the mischief-makers, the grandchildren, it seems, get along very nicely with the grandparents; and the sight of their concord points inevitably to the later breach between the generations, a breach more complete than the other, and perhaps more momentous. The failure of the Edwardians, comparative yet disastrous – that is a question which waits to be discussed. How the year 1860 was a year of empty cradles; how the reign of Edward the Seventh was barren of poet, novelist, or critic; how it followed that the Georgians read Russian novels in translations; how they benefited and suffered; how different a story we might have told today had there been living heroes to worship and destroy – all this we find significant in view of the new editions of the old books. The Georgians, it seems, are in the odd predicament of turning for solace and guidance not to their parents who are alive, but to their grandparents who are dead. And so, as likely as not, we shall be faced one of these days by a young man reading Meredith for the first time.

He has bought *Harry Richmond* and he is in the middle of it, and he is obviously annoyed when they come and ask him for his ticket. Is he not enviable? And what is it like, reading *Harry Richmond* for the first time? Let us try to remember. The book begins with a statue who turns out to be a man, and there is a preposterous adventurer, somehow descended from the Royal family, and there is a scene at a dinner-party, and a fire, and a dashing, impetuous girl, and a handsome manly boy, and England in June at night, and stars and rivers and love-making and gallantry. In short, the young man ought to be enjoying himself, and one of these days we will read *Harry Richmond* again. But there are difficulties to be faced. We do not mean that Meredith is said (perhaps not so truly) to be under a cloud. In our climate that is inevitable. But we mean that to read a novel for the second time is far more of an undertaking than to read it for the first. To rush it breathlessly through does very well for a beginning. But that is not the way to read finally; and somehow or other these fat Victorian volumes, these *Vanity Fairs*, *Copperfields*, *Richmonds*, and *Adam Bedes* must be read finally, if we are to do them justice – must be read as one reads *Hamlet*, as a whole. But, then, one reads *Hamlet* in the four hours between dinner and bedtime. It is not beyond human endurance to read it from first to last, in and out, and, so far as our faculties permit, as a whole. *Hamlet* may change; we know, indeed, that *Hamlet* will change; but tonight *Hamlet* is ours. And for that reason, too, we hesitate before reading *Harry Richmond* again. Tonight *Harry Richmond* will not be ours. We shall have broken off a tantalizing fragment: days may pass before we can add to it. Meanwhile the plan is lost; the book pours to waste; we blame ourselves; we abuse the author; nothing is more exasperating and dispiriting. Better leave the Victorian novelist to crumble on the shelves and be bolted whole by schoolboys. Let us confine ourselves to apt quotations from Mrs. Gamp, and find Hartfield on the map. Let us call Jane Austen 'Jane', and debate for ever which curate Emily Brontë loved. But the business of reading novels is beyond us, and there is nothing more melancholy than the sight of so many fine brains irrevocably expressed in the one form which makes them for ever inaccessible. So, instead of reading *Harry Richmond*, we will envy the young man opposite and wish Defoe and Fanny Burney at the bottom of the sea. They were the parents of the modern novel and their burden is heavy.

Some such mood of exasperation and bewilderment, of violence, yet of remorse, is abroad at present among those common readers whom Dr. Johnson respected, for it is by them, he said, that 'must be finally decided all claim to poetical honours'. It bodes ill for fiction if the commons of letters vote against it, so let us lay bare our dilemma without caring overmuch if we say some foolish things and many vague ones. To begin with, we have obviously got it into our heads that there is a right way to read, and that is to read straight through and grasp the book entire. The national habit has been formed by the drama, and the drama has always recognized the fact that human beings cannot sit for more than five hours at a stretch in front of a stage. And on top of that we are by temperament and tradition poetic. There still lingers among us the belief that poetry is the senior branch of the service. If we have an hour to spend we feel that we lay it out to better advantage with Keats than with Macaulay. And so perhaps we come to novels neither knowing the right way to read them nor very much caring to acquire it. We ask one thing and they give us another. They are so long, so dull, so badly written: and, after all, one has life enough on one's hands already without living it all over again between dinner and bedtime in prose. Such are the stock complaints, and they lose nothing of their acrimony if with the same breath we have to admit that we owe more to Tolstoy, Dostoevsky, and Hardy than we can measure; that if we wish to recall our happier hours they would be those Conrad has given us and Henry James; and that to have seen a young man bolting Meredith whole recalls the pleasure of so many first readings that we are even ready to venture a second. Only with these contrary impulses at work it will be a hazardous affair. Not again shall we be floated over on the tide of careless rapture. The pleasure we shall now look for will lie not so obviously on the surface; and we shall find ourselves hard pressed to make out what is the lasting quality, if such there be, which justifies these long books about modern life in prose. The collective reading of generations which has set us at the right angle for reading plays has not yet shaped our attitude to fiction. That *Hamlet* is a work of art goes without saying; but that *Harry Richmond* is a work of art has to be said for the first time.

Some months ago Mr. Percy Lubbock applied himself to answer some of these questions in *The Craft of Fiction* (Jonathan Cape. 9s. net), a book which is likely to have much influence upon readers, and may perhaps eventually reach the critics and writers. To say that it is the best book on the subject is probably true; but it is more to the point to say that it is the only one. He has attempted a task which has never been properly attempted, and has tentatively explored a field of inquiry which it is astonishing to find almost untilled. The subject is vast and the book short, but it will be our fault, not Mr. Lubbock's, if we talk as vaguely about novels in the future as we have done in the past. For example, do we say that we cannot read *Harry Richmond* twice? We are led by Mr. Lubbock to suspect that it was our first reading that was to blame. A strong but vague emotion, two or three characters, half a dozen scattered scenes – if that is all that *Harry Richmond* means to us, the fault lies, perhaps, not with Meredith, but with ourselves. Did we read the book as he meant it to be read, or did we not reduce it to chaos through our own incompetency? Novels, above all other books, we are reminded, bristle with temptations. We identify ourselves with this person or with that. We fasten upon the character or scene which is congenial. We swing our imaginations capriciously from spot to spot. We compare the world of fiction with the real world and judge it by the same standards. Undoubtedly we do all this, and easily find excuses for so doing. 'But meanwhile the book, the thing he made, lies imprisoned in the volume, and our glimpse of it was too fleeting, it seems, to leave us with a lasting knowledge of its form.' That is the point. There is something lasting that we can lay hands on. There is, Mr. Lubbock argues, such a thing as the book itself. We should read at arm's length from the distractions we have named. We must receive impressions, but we must relate them to each other as the author intended; and we can only do his bidding by making ourselves acquainted with his method. When we have shaped our impressions, as the author would have us, we are then in a position to perceive the form itself, and it is this which endures, however mood or fashion may change. In Mr. Lubbock's own words:

> But with the book in this condition of a defined shape, firm of outline, its form shows for what it is indeed – not an attribute, one of many and possibly not the most important, but the book itself, as the form of the statue is the statue itself.

Now as Mr. Lubbock laments, the criticism of fiction is in its infancy, and its language, though not all of one syllable, is baby language. This word 'form', of course, comes from the visual arts, and for our part we wish that he could have seen his way to do without it. It is confusing. The form of the novel differs from the dramatic form – that is true; we can, if we choose, say that we see the difference in our mind's eyes. But can we see that the form of *The Egoist* differs from the form of *Vanity Fair*? We do not raise the question in order to stickle for accuracy where most words are provisional, many metaphorical, and some on trial for the first time. The question is not one of words only. It goes deeper than that, into the very process of reading itself. Here we have Mr. Lubbock telling us that the book itself is equivalent to its form, and seeking with admirable subtlety and lucidity to trace out those methods by which novelists build up the final and enduring structure of their books. The very patness with which the image comes to the pen makes us suspect that it fits a little loosely. And in these circumstances it is best to shake oneself free from images and start afresh with a definite subject to work upon. Let us read a story and set down our impressions as we go along, and so perhaps discover what it is that bothers us in Mr. Lubbock's use of the word form. For this purpose there is no more appropriate author than Flaubert; and not to strain our space, let us choose a short story, 'Un Cœur Simple', for example, for, as it happens, it is one that we have practically forgotten.

The title gives us our bearings, and the first words direct our attention to Madame Aubain's faithful servant Félicité. And now the impressions begin to arrive. Madame's character; the look of her house; Félicité's appearance; her love affair with Théodore; Madame's children; her visitors; the angry bull. We accept them, but we do not use them. We lay them aside in reserve. Our attention flickers this way and that, from one to another. Still the impressions accumulate, and still, almost ignoring their individual quality, we read on, noting the pity, the irony, hastily observing certain relations and contrasts, but stressing nothing; always awaiting the final signal. Suddenly we have it. The mistress and the maid are turning over the dead child's clothes. 'Et des papillons s'envolèrent de l'armoire.' The mistress kisses the servant for the first time. 'Félicité lui en fut reconnaissante comme d'un bienfait, et désormais la chérit avec un dévouement bestial et une vénération religieuse.' A sudden intensity of phrase, something which for good reasons or for bad we feel to be emphatic, startles us into a flash of understanding. We see now why the story was written. Later in the same way we are roused by a sentence with a very different intention: 'Et Félicité priait en regardant l'image, mais de temps à autre se tournait un peu vers l'oiseau'. Again we have the same conviction that we know why the story was written. And then it is finished. All the observations which we have put aside now come out and range themselves according to the directions we have received. Some are relevant; others we can find no place for. On a second reading we are able to use our observations from the start, and they are much more precise; but they are still controlled by these moments of understanding.

Therefore the 'book itself' is not form which you see, but emotion which you feel, and the more intense the writer's feeling, the more exact without slip or chink its expression in words. And whenever Mr. Lubbock talks of form it is as if something were interposed between us and the book as we know it. We feel the presence of an alien substance which requires to be visualized imposing itself upon emotions which we feel naturally, and name simply, and range in final order by feeling their right relations to each other. Thus we have reached our conception of 'Un Cœur Simple' by working from the emotion outwards, and, the reading over, there is nothing to be seen; there is everything to be felt. And only when the emotion is feeble and the workmanship excellent can we separate what is felt from the expression and remark, for example, what excellence of form *Esther Waters* possesses in comparison with *Jane Eyre*. But consider the *Princesse de Clèves*. There is vision and there is expression. The two blend so perfectly that when Mr. Lubbock asks us to test the form with our eyes we see nothing at all. But we feel with singular satisfaction, and since all our feelings are in keeping, they form a whole which remains in our minds as the book itself. The point is worth labouring, not simply to substitute one word for another, but to insist among all this talk of methods, that both in writing and in reading it is the emotion that must come first.

Still, we have only made a beginning, and a very dangerous one at that. To snatch an emotion and luxuriate in it and tire of it and throw it away is as dissipating in literature as in life. Yet, if we wring this pleasure from Flaubert, the most austere of writers, there is no limit to be put upon the intoxicating effects of Meredith and Dickens and Dostoevsky, of Scott and Charlotte Brontë.

Or, rather, there is a limit, and we have found it over and over again in the extremes of satiety and distrust. If we are to read them a second time, we must somehow discriminate. Emotion is our material; but what do we mean by emotion? How many different kinds of emotion are there not in one short story, of how many qualities, and composed of how many different elements? And, therefore, to get our emotion directly, and for ourselves, is only the first step. We must go on to test it and riddle it with questions. If nothing survives, well and good; if something remains, all the better. The resolution is admirable; the only difficulty is how to enforce it. Did we thus wish to examine our impressions of some new play or poem, there are many dead, and five or six living, critics at whose command we cheerfully revise our views. But when it is fiction, and fiction hot from the press, far from accepting the judgment of any living critic or the applause or neglect of the public, we are forced, after competing half-a-dozen judgments, each based on a different conception of the art or on no conception at all, either to do the work for ourselves or to conclude that for some mysterious reason the work cannot be done. There may be something so emotional in fiction that the critics inevitably lose their heads. There may be something so unamenable to discipline in the art itself that it is hopeless either to judge it by the old standards or to devise new ones afresh. But now – at last – Mr. Lubbock applies his Röntgen rays. The voluminous lady submits to examination. The flesh, the finery, even the smile and witchery, together with the umbrellas and brown paper parcels which she has collected on her long and toilsome journey, dissolve and disappear; the skeleton alone remains. It is surprising. It is even momentarily shocking. Our old familiar friend has vanished. But, after all, there is something satisfactory in bone – one can grasp it.

In other words, by concentrating on the novelist's method, Mr. Lubbock draws our attention to the solid and enduring thing to which we can hold fast when we attack a novel for the second time. Here is something to which we can turn and turn again, and with each clearer view of it our understanding of the whole becomes more definite. Here is something removed (as far as may be) from the influence of our fluctuating and private emotions. The novelist's method is simply his device for expressing his emotion; but if we discover how that effect is produced we shall undoubtedly deepen the impression. Let us put it to the proof, since words are misleading. It is essential in 'Un Cœur Simple' that we should feel the lapse of time; the incidents are significant because they are scattered so sparsely over so long a stretch of years, and the effect must be given in a few short pages. So Flaubert introduces a number of people for no purpose, as we think; but later we hear that they are now all dead, and we realize then for how long

Félicité herself has lived. To realize that is to enforce the effect. It fastens our attention upon the story as a work of art, and gives us such a prise on it as we have already, thanks to their more rigid technique, upon drama and poetry, but have to contrive for fiction, afresh, each time we open a book.

But that is one detail in a short story. Can we sharpen our impressions of a long and crowded novel in the same way? Can we make out that the masters – Tolstoy and Flaubert, and Dickens, and Henry James, and Meredith – expressed by methods which we can trace and understand the enormous mass and the myriad detail of their books? If so the novel, the voluminous Victorian novel, is capable of being read, as we read *Hamlet*, as a whole. And the novelists, children of instinct, purveyors of illusion and distraction at the cheapest rates quoted in literature, are of the blood royal all the same. That is the conclusion to which Mr. Lubbock certainly brings us by means of an argument which is at once fascinating and strangely unfamiliar. We have been along the road so often and have wasted so many matches looking for signposts in dark corners. We must have been aware that a novelist, before he can persuade us that his world is real and his people alive, must solve certain questions and acquire certain skill. But until Mr. Lubbock pierced through the flesh and made us look at the skeleton we were almost ready to believe that nothing was needed but genius and ink. The novelists themselves have done little to open our eyes. They have praised the genius and blamed the ink, but they have never, with two famous exceptions, invited us in to see the process at work. Yet obviously there must be a process, and it is at work always and in every novel. The simplest story begins more often than not, as Mr. Lubbock points out, by the use of three different methods: the scene, the retrospect, the summary. And our innocence is gauged by the fact that though we swallow them daily it is with our eyes tight shut. Names have to be found and methods defined now for the first time.

No writer, indeed, has so many methods at his disposal as a novelist. He can put himself at any point of view; he can to some extent combine several different views. He can appear in person, like Thackeray; or disappear (never perhaps completely), like Flaubert. He can state the facts, like Defoe, or give the thought without the fact like Henry James. He can sweep the widest horizons, like Tolstoy, or seize upon one old apple-woman and her basket, like Tolstoy again. Where there is every freedom there is every licence; and the novel, open-armed, free to all comers, claims more victims than the other forms of literature all put together. But let us look at the victors. We are tempted, indeed, to look at them a great deal more closely than space allows. For they too look different if you watch them at work. There is Thackeray always taking measures to avoid a scene, and Dickens (save in *David Copperfield*) invariably seeking one. There is Tolstoy dashing into the midst of his story without staying to lay foundations, and Balzac laying foundations so deep that the story itself seems never to begin. But we must check the desire to see where Mr. Lubbock's criticism would lead us in reading particular books. The general view is more striking, and a general view is to be had.

Let us look not at each story separately, but at the method of story-telling – the use, that is, of each of these processes – which runs through them all. Let us look at it in Richardson's hands, and watch it changing and developing as Thackeray applies it, and Dickens and Tolstoy and Meredith and Flaubert and the rest. Then let us see how in the end Henry James, endowed not with greater genius but with greater knowledge and craftsmanship, surmounts in *The Ambassadors* problems which baffled Richardson in *Clarissa*. The view is difficult; the light is bad. At every angle someone rises to protest that novels are the outburst of spontaneous inspiration, and that Henry James lost as much by his devotion to art as he gained. We will not silence that protest, for it is the voice of an immediate joy in reading without which second readings would be impossible, for there would be no first. And yet the conclusion seems to us undeniable. Henry James achieved what Richardson attempted. 'The only real *scholar* in the art' beats the amateurs. The late-comer improves upon the pioneers. More is implied than we can even attempt to state.

For from that vantage ground the art of fiction can be seen, not clearly indeed, but in a new proportion. We may speak of infancy, of youth, and of maturity. We may say that Scott is childish and Flaubert by comparison a grown man. We may go on to say that the vigour and splendour of youth almost outweigh the more deliberate virtues of maturity. And then we may pause upon the significance of 'almost', and wonder whether, perhaps, it has not some bearing upon our reluctance to read the Victorians twice. The gigantic, sprawling books still seem to reverberate the yawns and lamentations of their makers. To build a castle, sketch a profile, fire off a poem, reform a workhouse, or pull down a prison were occupations more congenial to the writers, or more befitting their manhood, than to sit chained at a desk scribbling novels for a simple-minded public. The genius of Victorian fiction seems to be making its magnificent best of an essentially bad job. But it is never possible to say of Henry James that he is making the best of a bad job. In all the long stretch of *The Wings of the Dove* and *The Ambassadors* there is not the hint of a yawn, not a sign of condescension. The novel is his job. It is the appropriate form for what he has to say. It wins a beauty from that fact – a fine and noble beauty – which it has never worn before. And now at last (so we seem to see) the novel is a form distinct from any other. It will not burden itself with other people's relics. It will choose to say whatever it says best. Flaubert will take for his subject an old maid and a stuffed parrot. Henry James will find all he needs round a tea-table in a drawing-room. The nightingales and roses are banished – or at least the nightingale sounds strange against the traffic, and the roses in the light of the arc lamps are not quite so red. There are new combinations of old material and the novel, when it is used for the sake of its qualities and not for the sake of its defects, enforces fresh aspects of the perennial story.

Mr. Lubbock prudently carries his survey no further than the novels of Henry James. But already the years have mounted up. We may expect the novel to change and develop as it is explored by the most vigorous minds of a very complex age. What have we not, indeed, to expect from M. Proust alone? But if he will listen to Mr. Lubbock, the common reader will refuse to sit any longer open-mouthed in passive expectation. That is to encourage the charlatan to shock us and the conjuror to play us tricks. We must press close on his heels, and so bring to bear upon the novelist who spins his books in solitude the pressure of an audience. The pressure of an audience will not reduce the novel to a play which we can read through in the four hours between dinner and bedtime. But it will encourage the novelist to find out – and that is all we ask of him – what it is that he means and how best to show it us.

How it Strikes a Contemporary

In the first place a contemporary can scarcely fail to be struck by the fact that two critics at the same table at the same moment will pronounce completely different opinions about the same book. Here, on the right, it is declared a masterpiece of English prose; on the left, simultaneously, a mere mass of waste paper which, if the fire could survive it, should be thrown upon the flames. Yet both critics are in agreement about Milton and about Keats. They display an exquisite sensibility and have undoubtedly a genuine enthusiasm. It is only when they discuss the work of contemporary writers that they inevitably come to blows. The book in question, which is at once a lasting contribution to English literature and a mere farrago of pretentious mediocrity, was published about two months ago. That is the explanation; that is why they differ.

The explanation is a strange one. It is equally disconcerting to the reader who wishes to take his bearings in the chaos of contemporary literature and to the writer who has a natural desire to know whether his own work, produced with infinite pains and in almost utter darkness, is likely to burn for ever among the fixed luminaries of English letters or, on the contrary, to put out the fire. But if we identify ourselves with the reader and explore his dilemma first, our bewilderment is short-lived enough. The same thing has happened so often before. We have heard the doctors disagreeing about the new and agreeing about the old twice a year on the average, in spring and autumn, ever since Robert Elsmere, or was it Stephen Phillips, somehow pervaded the atmosphere, and there was the same disagreement among grown-up people about them. It would be much more marvellous and indeed much more upsetting, if, for a wonder, both gentlemen agreed, pronounced Blank's book an undoubted masterpiece, and thus faced us with the necessity of deciding whether we should back their judgment to the extent of ten and sixpence. Both are critics of reputation; the opinions tumbled out so spontaneously here will be starched and stiffened into columns of sober prose which will uphold the dignity of letters in England and America.

It must be some innate cynicism, then, some ungenerous distrust of contemporary genius, which determines us automatically as the talk goes on that, were they to agree – which they show no signs of doing – half a guinea is altogether too large a sum to squander upon contemporary enthusiasms, and the case will be met quite adequately by a card to the library. Still the question remains, and let us put it boldly to the critics themselves. Is there no guidance nowadays for a reader who yields to none in reverence for the dead, but is tormented by the suspicion that reverence for the dead is vitally connected with understanding of the living? After a rapid survey both critics are agreed that there is unfortunately no such person. For what is their own judgment worth where new books are concerned? Certainly not ten and sixpence. And from the stores of their experience they proceed to bring forth terrible examples of past blunders; crimes of criticism which, if they had been committed against the dead and not against the living, would have lost them their jobs and imperilled their reputations. The only advice they can offer is to respect one's own instincts, to follow them fearlessly and, rather than submit them to the control of any critic or reviewer alive, to check them by reading and reading again the masterpieces of the past.

Thanking them humbly, we cannot help reflecting that it was not always so. Once upon a time, we must believe, there was a rule, a discipline which controlled the great republic of readers in a way which is now unknown. That is not to say that the great critic – the Dryden, the Johnson, the Coleridge, the Arnold – was an impeccable judge of contemporary work, whose verdicts stamped the book indelibly and saved the reader the trouble of reckoning the value for himself. The mistakes of those great men about their own contemporaries are too notorious to be worth recording. But the mere fact of their existence had a centralizing influence. That alone, it is not fantastic to suppose, would have controlled the disagreements of the dinner table and given to random chatter about some book just out an authority now entirely to seek. The diverse schools would have debated as hotly as ever, but at the back of every reader's mind would have been the consciousness that there was at least one man who kept the main principles of literature closely in view: who, if you had taken to him some eccentricity of the moment, would have brought it into touch with permanence and tethered it by his own authority in the contrary blasts of praise and blame. But when it comes to the making of a critic, Nature must be generous and Society ripe. The scattered dinner tables of the modern world, the chase and eddy of the various currents which compose the Society of our time, could only be dominated by a giant of fabulous dimensions. And where is even the very tall man whom we have the right to expect? Critics, of course, abound. But the too frequent result of their able and industrious pens is a desiccation of the living tissues of literature into a network of little bones. Nowhere shall we find the downright vigour of Dryden, or Keats with his fine and natural bearing, or Flaubert and his fanaticism, or Coleridge, above all, brewing in his head the whole of poetry and letting issue now and then one of those profound general statements which are caught up by the mind when hot with the friction of reading as if they were of the soul of the book itself.

And to all this, too, the critics, generously, agree. A great critic, they say, is the rarest of beings. But should one miraculously appear, how should we maintain him, on what should we feed him? Great critics, if they are not themselves great poets, are bred from the profusion of the age. And our age is meagre to the verge of destitution. There is no name which dominates the rest, no master in whose workshop the young are proud to serve apprenticeship. Mr. Hardy has long since withdrawn from the arena, and there is something exotic about the genius of Mr. Conrad which makes him not so much an influence as an idol, honoured and admired, but aloof and apart. As for the rest, though they are many and vigorous and in the full flood of creative activity, there is none whose influence can seriously affect his contemporaries, or penetrate beyond our day to that not very distant future which it pleases us to call immortality. If we make a century our test, and ask how much of the work produced in these days in England will be in existence then, we shall have to answer not merely that we cannot agree upon the same book, but that we are more than doubtful whether such a book there is. It is an age of fragments. A few stanzas, a few pages, a chapter here and there, the beginning of this novel, the end of that, are equal to the best of any age or author. But can we go to posterity with a sheaf of loose pages, or ask the readers of those days, with the whole of literature before them, to sift our enormous rubbish heaps for our tiny pearls? To such questions it is fitting that a writer should reply; yet with what conviction?

At first the weight of pessimism seems sufficient to bear down all opposition. It is a lean age, we repeat, with much to justify its poverty; but, frankly, if we pit one century against another the comparison seems overwhelmingly against us. *Waverley*, *The Excursion*, *Kubla Khan*, *Don Juan*, Hazlitt's Essays, *Pride and Prejudice*, *Hyperion* and *Prometheus Unbound* were all published between 1800 and 1821. Our century has not lacked industry; but if we ask for masterpieces it appears on the face of it that the pessimists are right. It seems as if an age of genius must be succeeded by an age of endeavour; riot and extravagance by cleanliness and hard work. All honour, of course, to those who have sacrificed their immortality to set the house in order. But if we ask for masterpieces, where are we to look? A little poetry, we may feel sure, will survive; a few poems by Mr. Yeats, by Mr. Davies, by Mr. De la Mare. Mr. Lawrence, of course, has moments of greatness. Mr. Beerbohm in his way is perfect. Mr. Strachey paints portraits. Mr. Eliot makes phrases. Passages in *Far Away and Long Ago* will undoubt-edly go to posterity entire. *Ulysses* was a memorable catastrophe – immense in daring, terrific in disaster. And so, picking and choosing, we select now this, now that, hold it up for display, hear it defended or derided, and finally have to meet the objection that even so we are only agreeing with the critics that it is an age incapable of sustained effort, littered with fragments, and not seri-ously to be compared with the age that went before.

But it is just when opinions universally prevail and we have added lip service to their authority that we become sometimes most keenly conscious that we do not believe a word that we are saying. It is a barren and exhausted age, we repeat; we must look back with envy to the past. Meanwhile it is one of the first fine days of spring. Life is not altogether lacking in colour. The telephone, which interrupts the most serious conversations, has a romance of its own. And the random talk of people who have no chance of immortality and thus can speak their minds out has a setting, often, of lights, streets, houses, human beings, beautiful or grotesque, which will weave itself into the moment for ever. But this is life; the talk is about literature. We must try to disentangle the two, and justify the rash revolt of optimism against the superior plausibil-ity, the finer distinction, of pessimism. In one sense, of course, optimism is universal. No one would seriously choose to go back a hundred years. There is something about the present with all its trivialities which we would not exchange for the past, however august – just as an instinct, blind but essential to the conduct of life, makes every tramp prefer to be himself rather than any king, or hero, or millionaire of them all. And modern literature in spite of its imperfections has the same hold on us, the same endearing quality of being part of ourselves, of being the globe in which we are and not the globe which we look upon respectfully from outside. Nor has any generation more need than ours to cherish its contemporaries. We are sharply cut off from our predecessors. A shift in the scale – the war, the sudden slip of masses held in position for ages – has shaken the fabric from top to bottom, alienated us from the past and made us perhaps too vividly conscious of the present. Every day we find ourselves doing, saying, or thinking things that would have been impossible to our fathers. And we feel the differences which have not been noted far more keenly than the resemblances which have been very perfectly expressed. New books lure us to read them partly in the hope that they will reflect this re-arrangement of our attitude – those scenes, thoughts, and apparently fortuitous groupings of incongruous things which impinge upon us with so keen a sense of novelty – and, as literature does, give it back into our keeping whole and comprehended. Here indeed there is every reason for optimism. No age can have been more rich than ours in writers determined to give expression to the differences which separate them from the past and not to the resemblances which connect them with it. It would be invidious to mention names, but the most casual reader dipping into poetry, into fiction, into biography can hardly fail to be impressed by the courage, the sincerity, in a word by the widespread originality of our time. But our exhilaration is strangely curtailed. Book after book leaves us with the same sense of promise unachieved, of intellectual poverty, of brilliance which has been snatched from life but not transmuted into literature. Much of what is best in contemporary work has the appearance of being noted under pressure, taken down in a bleak shorthand which preserves with astonishing brilliance the movements and expressions of the figures as they pass across the screen. But the flash is soon over, and there remains with us a profound dissatisfaction. The irritation is as acute as the pleasure was intense.

Now, of course, is the time to correct these extremes of opinion by consulting, as the critics advise, the masterpieces of the past. We feel ourselves indeed driven to them, impelled not by calm judgment but by some imperious need to anchor our instability upon their security. But, honestly, the shock of the comparison between past and present is at first disconcerting. Undoubtedly there is a dullness in great books. There is an unabashed tranquillity in page after page of Wordsworth and Scott and

Miss Austen which is sedative to the verge of somnolence. Opportunities occur and they neglect them. Shades and subtleties accumulate and they ignore them. They seem deliberately to refuse to gratify those senses which are stimulated so briskly by the moderns; the senses of sight, of sound, of touch – above all, the sense of personality vibrating with perceptions which, since they are not generalized, but have their centre in some particular person at some precise moment, serve to make that person and that moment vivid to the utmost extreme. There is little of all this in the works of Wordsworth and Scott and Jane Austen. From what, then, arises that sense of security which gradually, delightfully, and completely overcomes us? It is the power of their belief – their conviction, that imposes itself upon us. In Wordsworth, the philosophic poet, this is obvious enough. But it is equally true of the careless Scott, who scribbled master-pieces to build castles before breakfast, and of the modest maiden lady who wrote furtively and quietly simply to give pleasure. In both there is the same natural conviction that life is of a certain quality. They have their judgment of conduct. They know the relations of human beings towards each other and towards the universe. Neither of them probably has a word to say about the matter outright. But everything depends on it. Only believe, we find ourselves saying, and all the rest will come of itself. Only believe, to take a very simple instance which the recent publication of *The Watsons* brings to mind, that a nice girl will instinctively try to soothe the feelings of a boy who has been snubbed at a dance, and then, if you believe it implicitly and unquestioningly, you will not only make people a hundred years later feel the same thing, but you will make them feel it as literature. For certainty of that kind is the condition which makes it possible to write. To believe that your impressions hold good for others is to be released from the cramp and confinement of personality. It is to be free, as Scott was free, to explore with a vigour which still holds us spellbound the whole world of adventure and romance. It is also the first step in that mysterious process in which Jane Austen was so great an adept. The little grain of experience being selected, believed in, and set outside herself, could be put precisely in its place, and she was then free to make it, by a process which never yields its secret to the analyst, into that complete statement which is literature.

So, then, our contemporaries afflict us because they have ceased to believe. The most sincere of them will only tell us what it is that happens to himself. They cannot make a world, because they are not free of other human beings. They cannot tell stories, because they do not believe that stories are true. They cannot generalize. They depend on their senses and emotions, whose testimony is trustworthy, rather than on their intellects, whose message is obscure. And they have perforce to deny themselves the use of some of the most powerful and some of the most exquisite of the weapons of their craft. Set down at a fresh angle of the eternal prospect, they can only whip out their notebooks and record with agonized intensity the flying gleams (which light on what?) and the transitory splendours, which may perhaps compose nothing whatever. The critics may well declare that if the age is indeed like this – and our vision is determined, of course, by our place at the table – then the risks of judging contemporary work are greater than ever before. There is every excuse for them if they are wide of the mark; and no doubt it would be better to retreat, as Matthew Arnold advised, from the burning ground of the present, 'of which the estimates are so often not only personal, but personal with passion', to the safe tranquillity of the past. But the note of pessimism jars. It is true that the writer of the present day must renounce his hope of making that complete statement which we call a masterpiece. He must be content to be a taker of notes. But if notebooks are perishable volumes, he may reflect that they are, after all, the stuff from which the masterpieces of the future are made. Truth, again, to speak in the manner of the myth-makers, has always been thus volatile, sometimes coming quietly into the open and suffering herself to be looked at, at others flying averted and obscured. But if she is the truth then we do well to watch for her most brief apparitions; and the sight of her will convince us that she is always the same, from Chaucer even to Mr. Conrad. The difference is on the surface; the continuity in the depths.

As for the critic, whose task it is to pass judgment on the books of the moment, let him think of them as the anonymous activities of free craftsmen working under the lash of no master, but obscurely, with ardour, and in the interest of a greater writer who is not yet born. Let him therefore be generous of encouragement, but chary of bestowing wreaths which fade and coronets which fall off. Let him see the present in relation to the future. Let him, in short, slam the door upon the cosy company where butter is plentiful and sugar cheap, and emulate rather that gaunt aristocrat, Lady Hester Stanhope, who kept a milk-white horse in her stable in readiness for the Messiah, and was for ever scanning the mountain tops, impatiently, but with confidence, for the first signs of His approach.

Montaigne

Once at Bar-le-Duc Montaigne saw a portrait which René King of Sicily had painted of himself, and asked, 'Why is it not, in like manner, lawful for everyone to draw himself with a pen, as he did with a crayon?' Offhand one might reply, Not only is it lawful but nothing could be easier. Other people may evade us, but our own features are almost too familiar. Let us begin. And then, when we attempt the task, the pen falls from our fingers; it is a matter of profound, mysterious, and overwhelming difficulty.

After all, in the whole of literature, how many people have succeeded in drawing themselves with a pen? Only Montaigne and Pepys and Rousseau perhaps. The *Religio Medici* is a coloured glass through which darkly one sees racing stars and a strange and turbulent soul. A bright polished mirror reflects the face of Boswell peeping between other people's shoulders in the famous biography. But this talking of oneself, following one's own vagaries, giving the whole map, weight, colour, and circumference of the soul, in its confusion, its variety, its imperfection – this art belonged to one man only: to Montaigne. As the centuries go by, there is always a crowd before that picture, gazing into its depths, seeing their own faces reflected in it, seeing more the longer they look, never being able to say quite what it is that they see. New editions testify to the perennial fascination. Here is the Navarre Society in England reprinting in five fine volumes Cotton's translation; while in France the firm of Louis Conard is issuing the complete works of Montaigne with the various readings in an edition to which Dr. Armaingaud has devoted a long lifetime of research.

To tell the truth about oneself, to discover oneself near at hand, is not easy.

> We hear of but two or three of the ancients who have beaten this road [said Montaigne]. No one since has followed the track; 'tis a rugged road, more so than it seems, to follow a pace so rambling and uncertain, as that of the soul; to penetrate the dark profundities of its intricate internal windings; to choose and lay hold of so many little nimble motions; 'tis a new and extraordinary undertaking; and that withdraws us from the common and most recommended employments of the world.

There is, in the first place, the difficulty of expression. We all indulge in the strange, pleasant process called thinking, but when it comes to saying, even to some one opposite, what we think, then how little we are able to convey! The phantom is through the mind and out of the window before we can lay salt on its tail, or slowly sinking and returning to the profound darkness which it has lit up momentarily with a wandering light. Face, voice, and accent eke out our words and impress their feebleness with character in speech. But the pen is a rigid instrument: it can say very little; it has all kinds of habits and ceremonies of its own. It is dictatorial too: it is always making ordinary men into prophets, and changing the natural stumbling trip of human speech into the solemn and stately march of pens. It is for this reason that Montaigne stands out from the legions of the dead with such irrepressible vivacity. We can never doubt for an instant that his book was himself. He refused to teach; he refused to preach; he kept on saying that he was just like other people. All his effort was to write himself down, to communicate, to tell the truth, and that is a 'rugged road, more than it seems'.

For beyond the difficulty of communicating oneself, there is the supreme difficulty of being oneself. This soul, or life within us, by no means agrees with the life outside us. If one has the courage to ask her what she thinks, she is always saying the very opposite to what other people say. Other people, for instance, long ago made up their minds that old invalidish gentlemen ought to stay at home and edify the rest of us by the spectacle of their connubial fidelity. The soul of Montaigne said, on the contrary, that it is in old age that one ought to travel, and marriage, which, rightly, is very seldom founded on love, is apt to become towards the end of life a formal tie better broken up. Again with politics, statesmen are always praising the greatness of Empire, and preaching the moral duty of civilizing the savage. But look at the Spanish in Mexico, cried Montaigne in a burst of rage. 'So many cities levelled with the ground, so many nations extermi-nated ... and the richest and most beautiful part of the world turned upside down for the traffic of pearl and pepper! Mechanic victories!' And then when the peasants came and told him that they had found a man dying of wounds and deserted him for fear lest justice might incriminate them, Montaigne asked:

> What could I have said to these people? 'Tis certain
> that this office of humanity would have brought
> them into trouble ... There is nothing so much nor
> so grossly, nor so ordinarily faulty as the laws.

Here the soul, getting restive, is lashing out at the more palpable forms of Montaigne's great bugbears, convention and ceremony. But watch her as she broods over the fire in the inner room of that tower which, though detached from the main building, has so wide a view over the estate. Really, she is the strangest creature to watch, far from heroic, variable as a weathercock, 'bashful, insolent; chaste, lustful; prating, silent; laborious, delicate; ingenious, heavy; melancholic, pleasant; lying, true; knowing, ignorant; liberal, covetous, and prodigal' – in short, so complex, so indefinite, corresponding so little to the version which does duty for her in public, that a man might spend his life merely in trying to run her to earth. The pleasure of the pursuit more than rewards one for any damage that it may inflict upon one's worldly prospects. The man who is aware of himself is henceforward independent; and he is never bored, and life is only too short, and he is steeped through and through with a profound yet temperate happiness. He alone lives, while other people, slaves of ceremony, let life slip past them in a kind of dream. Once conform, once do what other people do because they do it, and a lethargy steals over all the finer nerves and faculties of the soul. She becomes all outer show and inward emptiness; dull, callous, and indifferent.

Surely then, if we ask this great master of the art of life to tell us his secret, he will advise us to withdraw to the inner room of our tower and there turn the pages of books, pursue fancy after fancy as they chase each other up the chimney, and leave the government of the world to others. Retirement and contemplation – these must be the main elements of his prescription. But no; Montaigne is by no means explicit. It is impossible to extract a plain answer from that subtle, half smiling, half melancholy man, with the heavy-lidded eyes and the dreamy, quizzical expression. The truth is that life in the country, with one's books and vegetables and flowers, is often extremely dull. He could never see that his own green peas were so much better than other people's. Paris was the place he loved best in the whole world – 'jusques à ses verrues et à ses taches'. As for reading, he could seldom read any book for more than an hour at a time, and his memory was so bad that he forgot what was in his mind as he walked from one room to another. Book learning is nothing to be proud of, and as for the achievements of science, what do they amount to? He had always mixed with clever men, and his father had a positive veneration for them, but he had observed that, though they have their fine moments, their rhapsodies, their visions, the cleverest tremble on the verge of folly. Observe yourself: one moment you are exalted; the next a broken glass puts your nerves on edge. All extremes are dangerous. It is best to keep in the middle of the road, in the common ruts, however muddy. In writing choose the common words; avoid rhapsody and eloquence – yet poetry is delicious; the best prose of course is full of poetry.

It appears, then, that we are to aim at a democratic simplicity. We may enjoy our room in the tower, with the painted walls and the commodious bookcases, but down in the garden there is a man digging who buried his father this morning, and it is he and his like who live the real life and speak the real language. There is certainly an element of truth in that. Things are said very finely at the lower end of the table. There are perhaps more of the qualities that matter among the ignorant than among the learned. But again, what a vile thing the rabble is! 'the mother of ignorance, injustice, and inconstancy. Is it reasonable that the life of a wise man should depend upon the judgment of fools?' Their minds are weak, soft and without power of resistance. They must be told what it is expedient for them to know. It is not for them to face facts as they are. The truth can only be known by the well-born soul – 'l'âme bien née'. Who then are these well-born souls, whom we would imitate, if only Montaigne would enlighten us more precisely?

But no. 'Je n'enseigne poinct; je raconte.' After all how could he explain other people's souls when he could say nothing 'entirely simply and solidly, without confusion or mixture, in one word', about his own, when indeed it became daily more and more in the dark to him? One quality or principle there is perhaps – that one must not lay down rules. The souls whom one would wish to resemble, like Etienne de La Boétie, for example, are always the supplest. 'C'est estre, mais ce n'est pas vivre, que de se tenir attaché et oblige par necessité a un seul train.' The laws are mere conventions, utterly unable to keep touch with the vast variety and turmoil of human impulses; habits and customs are a convenience devised for the support of timid natures who dare not allow their souls free play. But we, who have a private life and hold it infinitely the dearest of our possessions, suspect nothing so much as an attitude. Directly we begin to protest, to attitudinize, to lay down laws, we perish. We are living for others, not for ourselves. We must respect those who sacrifice themselves in the public service, load them with honours, and pity them for allowing, as they must, the inevitable compromise; but for ourselves let us fly fame, honour, and all offices that put us under an obligation to others. Let us simmer over our incalculable cauldron, our enthralling confusion, our hotch-potch of impulses, our perpetual miracle – for the soul throws up wonders every second. Movement and change are the essence of our being; rigidity is death; conformity is death; let us say what comes into our heads, repeat ourselves, contradict ourselves, fling out the wildest nonsense, and follow the most fantastic fancies without caring what the world does or thinks or says. For nothing matters except life; and, of course, order.

This freedom, then, which is the essence of our being, has to be controlled. But it is difficult to see what power we are to invoke to help us, since every restraint of private opinion or public law has been derided; and Montaigne never ceases to pour scorn upon the misery, the weakness, the vanity of human nature. Perhaps, then, it will be well to turn to religion to guide us? 'Perhaps' is one of his favourite expressions; 'perhaps' and 'I think' and all those words which qualify the rash assumptions of human ignorance. Such words help one to muffle up opinions which it would be highly impolitic to speak outright. For one does not say everything; there are some things which at present it is advisable only to hint. One writes for a very few people, who understand. Certainly, seek the Divine guidance by all means, but meanwhile there is, for those who live a private life, another monitor, an invisible censor within, 'un patron au dedans', whose blame is much more to be dreaded than any other because he knows the truth; nor is there anything sweeter than the chime of his approval. This is the judge to whom we must submit; this is the censor who will help us to achieve that order which is the grace of a well-born soul. For 'C'est une vie exquise, celle qui se maintient en ordre jusques en son privé'. But he will act by his own light; by some internal balance will achieve that precarious and ever-changing poise which, while it controls, in no way impedes the soul's freedom to explore and experiment. Without other guide, and without precedent, undoubtedly it is far more difficult to live well the public life. It is an art which each must learn separately, though there are, perhaps, two or three men, like Homer, Alexander the Great, and Epaminondas among the ancients, and Etienne de La Boétie among the moderns, whose example may help us. But it is an art; and the very material in which it works is variable and complex and infinitely mysterious – human nature. To human nature we must keep close. '... il faut vivre entre les vivants.' We must dread any eccentricity or refinement which cuts us off from our fellow-beings. Blessed are those who chat easily with their neighbours about their sport or their buildings or their quarrels, and honestly enjoy the talk of carpenters and gardeners. To communicate is our chief business; society and friendship our chief delights; and reading, not to acquire knowledge, not to earn a living, but to extend our intercourse beyond our own time and province. Such wonders there are in the world; halcyons and undiscovered lands, men with dogs' heads and eyes in their chests, and laws and customs, perhaps, far superior to our own. Possibly we are asleep in this world; possibly there is some other which is apparent to beings with a sense which we now lack.

Here then, in spite of all contradictions, and qualifications, is something definite. These essays are an attempt to communicate a soul. On this point at least he is explicit.

It is not fame that he wants; it is not that men shall quote him in years to come; he is setting up no statue in the market-place; he wishes only to communicate his soul. Communication is health; communication is truth; communication is happiness. To share is our duty; to go down boldly and bring up to daylight the most hidden thoughts which are the most diseased; to conceal nothing; to pretend nothing; if we are ignorant, to say so; if we love our friends, to let them know it.

> ... car, comme je scay par une trop certaine expérience, il n'est aucune si douce consolation en la perte de nos amis que celle que nous aporte la science de n'avoir rieu oublié a leur dire et d'avoir eu avec eux une parfaite et entière communication.

There are people who when they travel wrap themselves up, 'se défandans de la contagion d'un air incogneu', in silence and suspicion. When they dine they must have the same food they get at home. Every sight and custom is bad unless it resembles those of their own village. They travel only to return. That is entirely the wrong way to set about it. We should start without any fixed idea where we are going to spend the night, or when we propose to come back; the journey is everything. Most necessary of all, but rarest good fortune, we should try to find before we start some man of our own sort who will go with us and to whom we can say the first thing that comes into our heads. For pleasure has no relish unless we share it. As for the risks – that we may catch a cold or get a headache – it is always worth while to risk a little illness for the sake of pleasure. 'Le plaisir est des principales espèces du profit.' Besides, if we do what we like, we always do what is good for us. Doctors and wise men may object, but let us leave doctors and wise men to their own dismal philosophy. For ourselves, who are ordinary men and women, let us return thanks to Nature for her bounty by using every one of the senses she has given us; vary our state as much as possible; turn now this side, now that, to the warmth, and relish to the full before the sun goes down the kisses of youth and the echoes of a beautiful voice singing Catullus. Every season is likeable, and wet days and fine, red wine and white, company and solitude. Even sleep, that deplorable curtailment of the joy of life, can be full of dreams; and the most common actions – a walk, a talk, solitude in one's own orchard – can be enhanced and lit up by the association of the mind. Beauty is everywhere, and beauty is only two fingers' breadth from goodness. So, in the name of health and sanity, let us not dwell on the end of the journey. Let death come upon us planting our cabbages, or on horseback, or let us steal away to some cottage and there let strangers close our eyes, for a servant sobbing or the touch of a hand would break us down. Best of all, let death find us at our usual occupations, among girls and good fellows, who make no protests, no lamentations; let him find us 'parmy les jeux, les festins, faceties, entretiens communs et populaires, et la musique, et des vers amoureux'. But enough of death; it is life that matters.

It is life that emerges more and more clearly as the essays reach, not their end, but their suspension in full career. It is life that becomes more and more absorbing as death draws near, one's self, one's soul, every fact of existence: that one wears silk stockings summer and winter; puts water in one's wine; has one's hair cut after dinner; must have a glass to drink from; has never worn spectacles; has a loud voice; carries a switch in one's hand; bites one's tongue; fidgets with one's feet; is apt to scratch one's ears; likes meat to be high; rubs one's teeth with a napkin (thank God, they are good!); must have curtains to one's bed; and, what is rather curious, began by liking radishes, then disliked them, and now likes them again. No fact is too little to let it slip through one's fingers and examine it; and, besides, there is the strange power we have in changing facts by the force of the imagination. Observe how the soul is always casting her own lights and shadows; makes the substantial hollow and the frail substantial; fills broad daylight with dreams; is as much excited by phantoms as by reality; and, in the moment of death, sports with a trifle. Observe too her duplicity, her complexity. She hears of a friend's loss and sympathizes, and yet has a bitter-sweet, malicious pleasure in the sorrows of others. She believes; at the same time she does not believe. Observe her extraordinary susceptibility to impressions, especially in youth. A rich man steals because his father kept him short of money as a boy. This wall one builds not for oneself, but because one's father loved such things. The soul is all laced about with nerves and sympathies which affect her every action, and yet even now, in 1580, no one has any clear knowledge – such cowards we are, such lovers of the smooth conventional ways – how she works or what she is except that of all things she is the most mysterious, and one's self the greatest monster and miracle in the world. '... plus je me hante et connois, plus ma difformité m'estonne, moins je m'entens en moy.' Observe, observe perpetually, and, so long as ink and paper exist, 'sans cesse et sans travail', Montaigne will write.

But there remains one final question which, if we could make him look up from his enthralling occupation, we should like to put to this great master of the art of life. In these extraordinary volumes of short and broken, long and learned, logical and contradictory statements we have heard the very pulse and rhythm of the soul, beating day after day, year after year, through a veil which, as time goes on, fines itself almost to nothing. Here is someone who succeeded in the hazardous enterprise of living, who served his country and lived retired; was landlord, husband, father; entertained kings, loved women, and mused for hours alone over old books. By means of perpetual experiment and observation of the subtlest he achieved at last a miraculous adjustment of all those wayward parts that constitute the human soul. He laid hold of the beauty of the world with all his fingers. He achieved happiness. If he had had to live again, he said he would have lived the same life over. But, as we watch with absorbed interest the enthralling spectacle of a soul living openly beneath our eyes, the question frames itself, Is pleasure the end of all? Whence this overwhelming interest in the nature of the soul? Why this overmastering desire to communicate with others? Is the beauty of this world enough or is there, elsewhere, some explanation of the mystery? But to this there is no answer, only one more question – 'Que sçais-je?'

Joseph Conrad

Suddenly, without giving us time to arrange our thoughts or prepare our phrases, our remarkable guest has left us; and his withdrawal without farewell or ceremony is in keeping with his mysterious arrival, long years ago, to take up his lodging in this country. For there was always an air of mystery about him. It was partly his Polish birth, partly his memorable appearance, partly his preference for living in the depths of the country out of ear-shot of gossips, beyond reach of hostesses, so that for news of him one had to depend upon the evidence of simple visitors with a habit of ringing door bells who reported of their unknown host that he had the most perfect manners, the brightest eyes, and spoke English with a strong foreign accent.

Still, though it is the habit of death to quicken and focus our memories, there clings to the genius of Conrad something essentially, and not accidentally, difficult of approach. His reputation of later years was, with one obvious exception, undoubtedly the highest in England;

yet he was not popular. He was read with passionate delight by some; others he left cold and lustreless. Among his readers were people of the most opposite ages and sympathies. Schoolboys of fourteen, driving their way through Marryat, Scott, Henty and Dickens, swallowed him down with the rest; while the seasoned and the fastidious, who in process of time have eaten their way to the heart of literature and there turn over and over a few precious crumbs, set Conrad scrupulously upon their banqueting table. One source of difficulty and disagreement is, of course, to be found where men have at all times found it, in his beauty. One opens his pages and feels as Helen must have felt when she looked in her glass and realized that, do what she would, she could never in any circumstances pass for a plain woman. So Conrad had been gifted, so he had schooled himself, and such was his obligation to a strange language wooed characteristically for its Latin qualities rather than its Saxon that it seems as if he neither would nor could make an ugly or insignificant movement of the pen. His mistress, his style, is a little somnolent sometimes in repose. But let somebody speak to her, and then how magnificently she bears down upon us, with what colour, triumph and majesty! Yet it is arguable that Conrad would have gained both in credit and in popularity if he had written what he had to write without this incessant care for appearances. They block and impede and distract, his critics say, pointing to those famous passages which it is becoming the habit to lift from their context and exhibit among other cut flowers of English prose. He was self-conscious and stiff and ornate, they complain, and the sound of his own voice was dearer to him than the voice of humanity in its anguish. The criticism is familiar, and as difficult to refute as the remarks of deaf people when *Figaro* is played. They see the orchestra; far off they hear a dismal scrape of sound; their own remarks are interrupted, and very naturally they conclude that the ends of life would be better served if instead of scraping Mozart those fifty fiddlers broke stones upon the road. That beauty teaches, that beauty is a disciplinarian, how are we to convince them, since her teaching is inseparable from the sound of her voice and to that they are deaf? But read Conrad, not in birthday books but in the bulk, and he must be lost indeed to the meaning of words who does not hear in that rather stiff and sombre music, with its reserve, its pride, its vast and implacable integrity, how it is better to be good than bad, how loyalty is good and honesty and courage, though ostensibly Conrad is concerned merely to show us the beauty of the night at sea. But it is ill work dragging such intimations from their element. Dried in our little saucers, without the magic and mystery of language, they lose their power to excite and goad; they lose the drastic power which is a constant quality of Conrad's prose.

For it was by virtue of something drastic in him, the qualities of a leader and captain, that Conrad kept his hold over boys and young people. Until *Nostromo* was written, his characters were fundamentally simple and heroic, as the young were quick to perceive, however subtle the mind and indirect the method of their creator. They were seafarers, used to solitude and silence. They were in conflict with Nature, but at peace with man. Nature was their antagonist; she it was who drew forth honour, magnanimity, loyalty, the qualities proper to man; she who in sheltered bays reared to womanhood beautiful girls unfathomable and austere. Above all it was Nature who turned out such gnarled and tested characters as Captain Whalley and old Singleton, obscure but glorious in their obscurity, who were to Conrad the pick of our race, whose praises he was never tired of celebrating:

> They had been strong as those are strong who know neither doubts nor hopes. They had been impatient and enduring, turbulent and devoted, unruly and faithful. Well-meaning people had tried to represent these men as whining over every mouthful of their food, as going about their work in fear of their lives. But in truth they had been men who knew toil, privation, violence, debauchery – but knew not fear, and had no desire of spite

in their hearts. Men hard to manage, but easy to inspire; voiceless men – but men enough to scorn in their hearts the sentimental voices that bewailed the hardness of their fate. It was a fate unique and their own; the capacity to bear it appeared to them the privilege of the chosen! Their generation lived inarticulate and indispensable, without knowing the sweetness of affections or the refuge of a home – and died free from the dark menace of a narrow grave. They were the everlasting children of the mysterious sea.

Such were the characters of the early books – *Lord Jim, Typhoon, The Nigger of the Narcissus, Youth*; and these books, in spite of the changes and fashions, are surely secure of their place among our classics. But they reach this height by means of qualities which the simple story of adventure, as Marryat told it, or Fenimore Cooper, has no claim to possess. For it is clear that to admire and celebrate such men and such deeds, romantically, wholeheartedly and with the fervour of a lover, one must be possessed of the double vision; one must be at once inside and out. To praise their silence one must possess a voice. To appreciate their endurance one must be sensitive to fatigue. One must be able to live on equal terms with the Whalleys and the Singletons and yet hide from their suspicious eyes the very qualities which enable one to understand them. Conrad alone was able to live that double life, for Conrad was compound of two men; together with the sea captain dwelt that subtle, refined, and fastidious analyst whom he called Marlow. 'A most discreet understanding man', he said of Marlow.

Marlow was one of those born observers who are happiest in retirement. Marlow liked nothing better than to sit on deck, in some obscure creek of the Thames, smoking and recollecting; smoking and speculating; sending after his smoke beautiful rings of words until all the summer's night became a little clouded with tobacco smoke. Marlow, too, had a profound respect for the men with whom he had sailed; but he saw the humour of them. He nosed out and described in masterly fashion those livid creatures who prey successfully upon the clumsy veterans. He had a flair for human deformity; his humour was sardonic. Nor did Marlow live entirely wreathed in the smoke of his own cigars. He had a habit of opening his eyes suddenly and looking – at a rubbish heap, at a port, at a shop counter – and then complete in its burning ring of light that thing is flashed upon the mysterious background. Introspective and analytical, Marlow was aware of this peculiarity. He said the power came to him suddenly. He might, for instance, overhear a French officer murmur '*Mon Dieu*, how the time passes!'

Nothing [he comments] could have been more commonplace than this remark; but its utterance coincided for me with a moment of vision. It's extraordinary how we go through life with eyes half shut, with dull ears, with dormant thoughts ... Nevertheless, there can be but few of us who had never known one of these rare moments of awakening, when we see, hear, understand, ever so much – everything – in a flash, before we fall back again into our agreeable somnolence. I raised my eyes when he spoke, and I saw him as though I had never seen him before.

Picture after picture he painted thus upon that dark background; ships first and foremost, ships at anchor, ships flying before the storm, ships in harbour; he painted sunsets and dawns; he painted the night; he painted the sea in every aspect; he painted the gaudy brilliancy of Eastern ports, and men and women, their houses and their attitudes. He was an accurate and unflinching observer, schooled to that 'absolute loyalty towards his feelings and sensations', which, Conrad wrote, 'an author should keep hold of in his most exalted moments of creation'. And very quietly and compassionately Marlow sometimes lets fall a few words of epitaph which remind us, with all that beauty and brilliancy before our eyes, of the darkness of the background.

Thus a rough and ready distinction would make us say that it is Marlow who comments, Conrad who creates. It would lead us, aware that we are on dangerous ground, to account for that change which, Conrad tells us, took place when he had finished the last story in the *Typhoon* volume – 'a subtle change in the nature of the inspiration' – by some alteration in the relationship of the two old friends. '... it seemed somehow that there was nothing more in the world to write about.' It was Conrad, let us suppose, Conrad the creator, who said that, looking back with sorrowful satisfaction upon the stories he had told; feeling as he well might that he could never better the storm in *The Nigger of the Narcissus*, or render more faithful tribute to the qualities of British seamen than he had done already in *Youth* and *Lord Jim*. It was then that Marlow the commentator reminded him how, in the course of nature, one must grow old, sit smoking on deck, and give up seafaring. But, he reminded him, those strenuous years had deposited their memories; and he even went so far perhaps as to hint that, though the last word might have been said about Captain Whalley and his relation to the universe, there remained on shore a number of men and women whose relationships, though of a more personal kind, might be worth looking into. If we further suppose that there was a volume of Henry James on board and that Marlow gave his friend the book to take to bed with him, we may seek support in the fact that it was in 1905 that Conrad wrote a very fine essay upon that master.

For some years then it was Marlow who was the dominant partner. *Nostromo, Chance, The Arrow of Gold* represent that stage of the alliance which some will continue to find the richest of all. The human heart is more intricate than the forest, they will say; it has its storms; it has its creatures of the night; and if as novelist you wish to test man in all his relationships, the proper antagonist is man; his ordeal is in society, not solitude. For them there will always be a peculiar fascination in the books where the light of those brilliant eyes falls not only upon the waste of waters but upon the heart in its perplexity. But it must be admitted that, if Marlow thus advised Conrad to shift his angle of vision, the advice was bold. For the vision of a novelist is both complex and specialized; complex because behind his characters and apart from them must stand something stable to which he relates them; specialized because since he is a single person with one sensibility the aspects of life in which he can believe with conviction are strictly limited. So delicate a balance is easily disturbed. After the middle period Conrad never again was able to bring his figures into perfect relation with their background. He never believed in his later and more highly sophisticated characters as he had believed in his early seamen; because when he had to indicate their relation to that other unseen world of the novelists, the world of values and convictions, he was far less sure what those values were. Then, over and over again, a single phrase, 'He steered with care', coming at the end of a storm, carried in it a whole morality. But in this more crowded and complicated world such terse phrases became less and less appropriate. Complex men and women of many interests and relations would not submit to so summary a judgment; or, if they did, much that was important in them escaped the verdict. And yet it was very necessary to Conrad's genius, with its luxuriant and romantic power, to have some law by which its creations could be tried. Essentially – such remained his creed – this world of civilized and self-conscious people is based upon 'a few very simple ideas'; but where, in the world of thoughts and personal relations, are we to find them? There are no masts in drawing rooms; the typhoon does not test the worth of politicians and business men. Seeking and not finding such supports, the world of Conrad's later period has about it an involuntary obscurity, an inconclusiveness, almost a disillusionment which baffles and fatigues. We lay hold in the dusk only of the old nobilities and sonorities: fidelity, compassion, honour, service – beautiful always, but now a little wearily reiterated, as if times had changed. Perhaps it was Marlow who was at fault. His habit of mind was a trifle sedentary. He had sat upon deck too long; splendid in soliloquy, he was less apt in the give and take of conversation; and those 'moments of vision', flashing and fading, do not serve as well as steady lamplight to illumine the ripple of life and its long, gradual years. Above all, perhaps he did not take into account how, if Conrad was to create, it was essential first that he should believe.

Therefore, though we shall make expeditions into the later books and bring back wonderful trophies, large tracts of them will remain by most of us untrodden. It is the earlier books – *Youth*, *Lord Jim*, *Typhoon*, *The Nigger of the Narcissus* – that we shall read in their entirety. For when the question is asked, what of Conrad will survive and where in the ranks of novelists we are to place him, these books, with their air of telling us something very old and perfectly true which had lain hidden but is now revealed, will come to mind and make such questions and comparisons seem a little futile. Complete and still, very chaste and very beautiful, they rise in the memory as, on these hot summer nights, in their slow and stately way first one star comes out and then another.

Notes on an Elizabethan Play

There are, it must be admitted, some highly formidable tracts in English literature: and chief among them that jungle, forest, and wilderness which is the Elizabethan drama. For many reasons, not here to be examined, Shakespeare stands out: Shakespeare, who has had the light on him from his day to ours; Shakespeare, who towers highest when looked at from the level of his own contemporaries. But the plays of the lesser Elizabethans – Greene, Dekker, Peele, Chapman, Beaumont and Fletcher – to adventure into that wilderness is for the ordinary reader an ordeal, an upsetting experience which plies him with questions, harries him with doubts, alternately delights and vexes him with pleasures and pains. For we are apt to forget, reading, as we tend to do, only the masterpieces of a bygone age, how great a power the body of a literature possesses to impose itself: how it will not suffer itself to be read passively, but takes us and rends us; flouts our preconceptions, questions principles which we had got into the habit of taking for granted, and in fact splits us into two parts as we read, making us, even as we enjoy, yield our ground or stick to our guns.

At the outset in reading an Elizabethan play we are overcome by the extraordinary discrepancy between the Elizabethan view of reality and our own. The reality to which we have grown accustomed is, speaking roughly, based upon the life and death of some knight called Smith, who succeeded his father in the family business of pitwood importers, timber merchants and coal exporters, was well known in political, temperance, and Church circles, did much for the poor of Liverpool, and died last Wednesday of pneumonia while on a visit to his son at Muswell Hill. That is the world we know. That is the reality which our poets and novelists have to expound and illuminate. Then we open the first Elizabethan play that comes to hand and read how

> I once did see
> In my young travels through Armenia
> An angry unicorn in his full career
> Charge with too swift a foot a jeweller
> That watch'd him for the treasure of his brow
> And ere he could get shelter of a tree
> Nail him with his rich antlers to the earth.

Where is Smith, we ask; where is Liverpool? And the groves of Elizabethan drama echo 'Where?' Exquisite is the delight, sublime the relief, of being set free to wander in the land of the unicorn and the jeweller, among dukes and grandees, Gonzaloes and Bellimperias, who spend their lives in murder and intrigue, dress up as men if they are women, as women if they are men, see ghosts, run mad, and die in the greatest profusion on the slightest provocation, uttering, as they fall, imprecations of superb vigour or elegies of the wildest despair. But soon the low, the relentless, voice which, if we wish to identify it, we must suppose typical of a reader fed on modern English literature, and French and Russian, asks why, then, with all this to stimulate and enchant, these old plays are for long stretches of time so intolerably dull? Is it not that literature, if it is to keep us on the alert through five acts or thirty-two chapters, must somehow be based on Smith, have one toe touching Liverpool, take off into whatever heights it pleases from reality? We are not so purblind as to suppose that a man, because his name is Smith and he lives at Liverpool, is therefore 'real'. We know indeed that this reality is a chameleon quality: the fantastic becoming as we grow used to it often the closest to the truth, the sober the farthest from it, and nothing proving a writer's greatness more than his capacity to consolidate his scene by the use of what, until he touched them, seemed wisps of cloud and threads of gossamer.

Our contention merely is that there is a station, some-where in mid air, whence Smith and Liverpool can be seen to the best advantage; that the great artist is the man who knows where to place himself above the shifting scenery; that, while he never loses sight of Liverpool, he never sees it in the wrong perspective. The Elizabethans bore us, then, because their Smiths are all changed to dukes, their Liverpools to fabulous islands and palaces in Genoa. Instead of keeping a proper poise above life, they soar miles into the empyrean, where nothing is visible for long hours at a time but clouds at their revelry; and a cloud landscape is not ultimately satisfactory to human eyes. The Elizabethans bore us because they suffocate our imaginations rather than set them to work.

Still, though potent enough, the boredom of an Elizabethan play is of a different quality altogether from the boredom which a nineteenth-century play, a Tennyson or a Henry Taylor play, inflicts. The riot of images, the violent volubility of language, all that cloys and satiates in the Elizabethans, nevertheless appears to be drawn up with a roar, as a feeble fire is sucked up by a newspaper. There is, even in the worst, an intermittent bawling vigour which gives us the sense, in our quiet arm-chairs, of ostlers and orange girls catching up the lines, flinging them back, hissing or stamping applause. But the deliberate drama of the Victorian age is evidently written in a study. It has for audience ticking clocks and rows of classics bound in half morocco. There is no stamping, no applause. With all its faults – its patriotism, rhetoric and bombast – the Elizabethan audience leavened the mass with fire. The lines are flung and hurried into existence and reach the same impromptu felicities, have the same lip-moulded profusion and unexpectedness which speech sometimes achieves, but seldom, in our day, the deliberate, solitary pen. Indeed, half the work of dramatists, one feels, was done in the Elizabethan age by the public.

Against that, however, is to be set the fact that the influence of the public was in many respects detestable. To its door we must lay the greatest infliction that Elizabethan drama puts upon us – the plot; the incessant, improbable, almost unintelligible convolutions which presumably gratified the spirit of an excitable and unlettered public actually in the playhouse, but only confuse and fatigue a reader with the book before him. Undoubtedly something must happen; undoubtedly a play where nothing happens is an impossibility. But we have a right to demand (since the Greeks have proved that it is perfectly possible) that what happens shall have an end in view. It shall agitate great emotions, bring into existence memorable scenes, stir the actors to say what could not be said without this stimulus. Nobody can fail to remember the plot of the *Antigone* because what happens is so closely bound up with the emotions of the actors that we remember the people and the plot at one and the same time. But who can tell us what happens in *The White Devil*, or in *The Maid's Tragedy*, except by remembering the story apart from the emotions which it has aroused? As for the lesser Elizabethans, like Greene and Kyd, the complexities of their plots are so great, and the violence which these plots demand so terrific, that the actors themselves are obliterated, and emotions which, according to our convention, deserve the most careful investigation, the most delicate analysis, are clean sponged off the slate. And the result is inevitable. Outside Shakespeare and perhaps Ben Jonson, there are no characters in Elizabethan drama; only violences whom we know so little that we can scarcely care what becomes of them. Take any hero or heroine in those early plays – Bellimperia in *The Spanish Tragedy* will serve as well as another – and can we honestly say that we care a jot for the unfortunate lady who runs the whole gamut of human misery to kill herself in the end? No more than for an animated broomstick, we must reply; and in a work dealing with men and women the prevalence of broomsticks is a drawback. But *The Spanish Tragedy* is admittedly a crude forerunner, chiefly valuable because such primitive efforts lay bare the formidable framework which greater dramatists could modify but had to use. Ford, it is claimed, is of the school of Stendhal and of Flaubert. Ford is a psychologist. Ford is an analyst. 'This man', says

Mr. Havelock Ellis, 'writes of women not as a dramatist nor as a lover but as one who has searched intimately and felt with instinctive sympathy the fibres of their hearts.'

The play – *'Tis Pity She's a Whore* – upon which this judgment is chiefly based shows us the whole nature of Annabella spun from pole to pole in a series of tremendous vicissitudes. First her brother tells her that he loves her; next she confesses her love for him; next finds herself with child by him; next forces herself to marry Soranzo; next is discovered; next repents; finally is killed, and it is her lover and brother who kills her. To trace the trail of feelings which such crises and calamities might be expected to breed in a woman of ordinary sensibility might have filled volumes. A dramatist, of course, has no volumes to fill. He is forced to contract. Even so, he can illumine; he can reveal enough for us to guess the rest. But what is it that we know, without using microscopes and splitting hairs, about the character of Annabella? Gropingly we make out that she is a spirited girl, with her defiance of her husband when he abuses her, her snatches of Italian song, her ready wit, her simple glad love-making. But of character as we understand the word there is no trace. We do not know how she reaches her conclusions, only that she has reached them. Nobody describes her. She is always at the height of her passion, never at its approach. Compare her with Anna Karenina. The Russian woman is flesh and blood, nerves and temperament, has heart, brain, body, and mind, where the English girl is flat and crude as a face painted on a playing card; she is without depth, without range, without intricacy. But as we say this we know that we have missed something. We have let the meaning of the play slip through our hands. We have ignored the emotion which has been accumulating, because it has accumulated in places where we have not expected to find it. We have been comparing the play with prose, and the play, after all, is poetry.

The play is poetry, we say, and the novel prose. Let us attempt to obliterate detail, and place the two before us side by side, feeling, so far as we can, the angles and edges of each, recalling each, so far as we are able, as a whole. Then at once the prime differences emerge: the long, leisurely accumulated novel; the little contracted play: the emotion all split up, woven together slowly, and gradually massed into a whole in the novel; the emotion concentrated, generalized, heightened in the play. What moments of intensity, what phrases of astonishing beauty the play shot at us!

> O my lords
> I but deceived your eyes with antic gesture,
> When one news straight came huddling on another
> Of death! and death! and death! still I danced
> > forward.

Or

> You have oft for these two lips
> Neglected cassia or the natural sweets
> Of the spring-violet: they are not yet much
> > wither'd.

With all her reality, Anna Karenina could never say

> You have oft for these two lips
> Neglected cassia.

Some of the most profound of human emotions are therefore beyond her reach. The extremes of passion are not
for the novelist; the perfect marriages of sense and sound
are not for him: he must tame his swiftness to sluggardry,
keep his eyes on the ground, not on the sky: suggest by
description, not reveal by illumination. Instead of
singing

> Lay a garland on my hearse
> > Of the dismal yew;
> Maidens, willow branches bear;
> > Say I died true,

he must enumerate the chrysanthemums fading on the grave and the undertakers' men snuffling past in four-wheelers. How then can we compare this lumbering and lagging art with poetry? Granted all the little dexterities by which the novelist makes us know the individual and recognize the real, the dramatist goes beyond the single and the separate: shows us not Annabella in love, but love itself; not Anna Karenina throwing herself under the train, but ruin and death and the

> soul like a ship in a black storm,
> ... driven I know not whither.

So with pardonable impatience we might exclaim as we shut our Elizabethan play. But what then is the exclamation with which we close *War and Peace*? Not one of disappointment; we are not left lamenting the superficiality, upbraiding the triviality, of the novelist's art. Rather we are made more than ever aware of the inexhaustible richness of human sensibility. Here, in the play, we recognize the general; here, in the novel, the particular. Here we gather all our energies into a bunch and spring. Here we extend and expand and let come slowly in from all quarters deliberate impressions, accumulated messages. The mind is so saturated with sensibility, language so inadequate to its experience, that, far from ruling off one form of literature or decreeing its inferiority to others, we complain that they are still unable to keep pace with the wealth of material, and wait impatiently the creation of what may yet be devised to liberate us of the enormous burden of the unexpressed.

Thus in spite of dullness, bombast, rhetoric, and confusion, we still read the lesser Elizabethans, still find ourselves adventuring in the land of the jeweller and the unicorn. The familiar factories of Liverpool fade into thin air, and we scarcely recognize any likeness between the knight who imported timber and died of pneumonia at Muswell Hill and the Armenian duke who fell like a Roman on his sword while the owl shrieked in the ivy and the duchess gave birth to a still-born babe 'mongst women howling. To join these territories and recognize the same man in different disguise we have to adjust and revise. But make the necessary alterations in perspective, draw in those filaments of sensibility which the moderns have so marvellously developed, use instead the ear and the eye which the moderns have so basely starved, hear words as they are laughed and shouted, not as they are printed in black letters on the page, see before your eyes the changing faces and living bodies of men and women – put yourself, in short, into a different but not more elementary stage of your reading development – and then the true merits of Elizabethan drama will assert themselves. The power of the whole is undeniable. Theirs, too, is the word-coining genius, as if thought plunged into a sea of words and came up dripping. Theirs is the broad humour which was possible when the body was naked; impossible, however arduously the public-spirited may try, since the body is draped.

Then at the back of this, imposing not unity but some sort of stability, is what we may briefly call a sense of the presence of the gods. He would be a bold critic who should attempt to impose any creed upon the swarm and variety of the Elizabethan dramatists; and yet it implies some timidity if we take it for granted that a whole litera-ture with common characteristics is a mere evaporation of high spirits, a money-making enterprise, a fluke of the mind which, owing to favourable circumstances, came off successfully. Even in the jungle and the wilderness the compass still points.

> Lord, lord, that I were dead!

they are for ever crying:

> O thou soft natural death that art joint-twin
> To sweetest slumber –

The pageant of the world is marvellous, but the pageant of the world is vanity –

> glories
> Of human greatness are but pleasing dreams
> And shadows soon decaying: on the stage
> Of my mortality my youth hath acted
> Some scenes of vanity.

To die and be quit of it all is their desire; the bell that tolls throughout the drama is death and disenchantment:

> All life is but a wandering to find home,
> When we're gone, we're there.

Ruin, weariness, death, perpetually death, stand grimly to confront the other presence of Elizabethan drama, which is life: life compact of frigates, fir trees, and ivory; of dolphins and the juice of July flowers; of the milk of unicorns and panthers' breath; of ropes of pearl, brains of peacocks, and Cretan wine. To this, life at its most reckless and abundant, they reply

> Man is a tree that hath no top in cares,
> No root in comforts; all his power to live
> Is given to no end but t'have power to grieve.

It is this echo flung back and back from the other side of the play which, if it has not the name, still has the effect of the presence of the gods.

So we ramble through the jungle, forest, and wilderness of Elizabethan drama. So we consort with emperors and clowns, jewellers and unicorns, and laugh and exult and marvel at the splendour and humour and fantasy of it all. A noble rage consumes us when the curtain falls; we are bored too, and nauseated by the wearisome old tricks and florid bombast. A dozen deaths of full-grown men and women move us less than the suffering of one of Tolstoy's flies. Wandering almost suffocated in the maze of the impossible and tedious story, suddenly some passionate intensity seizes us; some sublimity exalts, or some melodious snatch of song enchants. It is a world full of tedium and delight, pleasure and curiosity; of extravagant laughter, poetry and splendour. But gradually it comes over us, What then are we being denied? What is it that we are coming to want so persistently that unless we get it instantly we must seek elsewhere? It is solitude. There is no privacy here. Always the door opens and some one comes in. All is shared, made visible, audible, dramatic. Meanwhile, as if tired with company, the mind steals off to muse in solitude; to think, not to act; to comment, not to share; to explore its own darkness, not the bright lit up surfaces of others. It turns to Donne, to Montaigne, to Sir Thomas Browne – all keepers of the keys of solitude.

Thomas Hardy's Novels

When we say that the death of Thomas Hardy leaves the art of fiction in England without a head we are speaking the most obvious of truths. So long as Hardy lived there was not a writer who did not feel that his calling was crowned by the unworldly and simple old man who made not the slightest effort to assert his sovereignty, yet stood for more to this generation than it is possible for any single voice to say. The effect of such a presence is indeed incalculable. His greatness as a writer, his standing among the great of other ages, will be judged perhaps more truly by critics of a later day. But it is for the living to bear witness to another sort of influence, hardly less important, though bound in the nature of things more quickly to disappear. His was a spiritual force; he made it seem honourable to write, desirable to write with sincerity; so long as he lived there was no excuse for thinking meanly of the art he practised. His genius, his age, his distance might remove all possibility of intercourse; the plainness and homeliness of his life lent him an obscurity which neither legend nor gossip disturbed; but it is no exaggeration to say that while he lived there was a king among us and now we are without. Of no one, however, would it be more unfitting to write in terms of rhetorical eulogy. His only demand upon us, and there is none more exacting, was that we should speak the truth.

Our task, then, as we consider the seventeen volumes of fiction which he has left us, is not to attempt to grade them in order of merit or to assign them to their final station in English literature. Rather we must try to discover the broad outlines of his genius, to distinguish between those qualities which are and those which are not still forces in the life of the present moment, to content ourselves with conjectures rather than attempt the more exact and measured estimate which time will bring within our reach. Let us go back to the beginning, to the year 1871, to the first novel, *Desperate Remedies*, and make our starting point there. Here is a young man, as he says in his preface, 'feeling his way to a method'; a young man of powerful imagination and of sardonic turn; book-learned in a home-made way; who can create characters but cannot control them; obviously hampered by the difficulties of his technique, and driven, both by maladroitness and by an innate desire to pit his human figures against forces outside themselves, to shape his book by an extreme and even desperate use of coincidence. He is already possessed of the conviction that a novel is not a toy, or an argument, but can deal faithfully with life, and record a truthful, if not a pleasing, account of the destinies of men and women. Had there been in those days a critic of abnormal perspicacity he might have said that the most remarkable thing in this first book was not character or plot or humour, but the sound that echoed and boomed through its pages of a waterfall. It is the first manifestation of that power which was to grow to such huge dimensions later. It is not the power of observing nature, though already Hardy knew how the rain falls differently on roots and arable, how the wind sounds differently through the branches of different trees; it is the power of making a symbol of nature, of summoning a spirit from down or mill-wheel or moor which can sympathize or can mock or can remain a passive and indifferent spectator of the drama of man. Already that gift was his; already in this crude story the involved fortunes of Miss Aldclyffe and Cytherea are watched by the eyes of the gods and worked out in the presence of nature. That he was a poet should have been obvious; that he was a novelist might still have been held uncertain. But the year after, when *Under the Greenwood Tree* appeared, it was clear that much of the effort of 'feeling for a method' had been overcome. Something of the stubborn originality of the earlier book was lost. The second is accomplished, charming, idyllic compared with the first. The writer, it seems, may well develop into one of our English landscape painters, whose pictures are all of cottage gardens and old peasant women, who lingers to collect and preserve from oblivion the old-fashioned ways and words which are rapidly falling into disuse. And yet what kindly lover of antiquity, what naturalist with a microscope in his pocket, what scholar solicitous for the changing shapes of language, ever heard the cry of a small bird killed in the next wood by an owl with such intensity? The cry 'passed into the silence without mingling with it'. Again we hear, very far away like the sound of a gun out at sea on a calm summer's morning, a strange and ominous echo. But as we read these early books there is a sense of waste. There is a feeling that Hardy's genius was obstinate and perverse; first one gift would have its way with him and then another. They would not consent to run together easily in harness. Such indeed was likely to be the fate of a writer who was at once poet and realist, a faithful son of field and down, yet tormented by the doubts and despondencies bred of book-learning; a lover of old ways and plain countrymen, yet doomed to see the faith and flesh of his forefathers turn to thin and spectral transparencies before his eyes.

To this contradiction nature had added another element likely to disorder a symmetrical development. Some writers (as readers we know it, though as critics we may fail to explain it) are born conscious of everything, others unconscious of many things. Some, like Henry

James and Flaubert, are able not merely to make the best use of the spoil their gifts bring in, but beyond that they control their genius in the act of creation, they remain aware and awake and are never taken by surprise. The unconscious writers, on the other hand, like Dickens and Scott, seem suddenly and without their own consent to be lifted up and swept onwards. The wave sinks and they cannot say what has happened or why. Among them – it is the source of his strength and the source of his weakness – we must place Hardy. His own word, 'moments of vision', exactly describes those passages of astonishing beauty and force which are to be found in every book that he wrote. With a sudden quickening of power which we cannot foretell, nor he, it seems, control, a single scene breaks off from the rest. We see, as if it existed alone and for all time, the wagon with Fanny's dead body inside travelling along the road under the dripping trees; we see the bloated sheep struggling among the clover; we see Troy flashing his sword round Bathsheba where she stands motionless, cutting the lock off her head and spitting the caterpillar on her breast. Vivid to the eye, but not to the eye alone, for every sense participates, such scenes dawn upon us and their splendour remains. But the power goes as it comes. The moment of vision is succeeded by long stretches of plain daylight, nor can we believe that any craft or skill could have caught the wild power and turned it to the best advantage. The novels therefore are full of inequalities; they are hewn rather than polished; and there is always about them that little blur of unconsciousness, that halo of freshness and margin of the unexpressed which often produce the most profound sense of satisfaction. It is as if Hardy himself were not quite aware of what he did, as if his conscious-ness held more than he could produce, and he left it for his readers to make out his full meaning and to supple-ment it from their own experience.

For these reasons Hardy's genius was uncertain in development, uneven in accomplishment, but when the moment came, magnificent in achievement. The moment came, completely and fully, in *Far from the Madding Crowd*. The subject was right; the method was right; the poet and the countryman, the sensual man, the sombre reflective man, the man of learning, all enlisted to produce a book which, however fashions may chop and change, must remain one of the great English novels. There is, in the first place, that sense of the physical world which Hardy more than any novelist can bring before us; the sense that the little prospect of man's exist-ence is ringed by a landscape which, while it exists apart, yet confers a deep and solemn beauty upon his drama. The dark downland, marked by the barrows of the dead and the huts of shepherds, rises against the sky, smooth as a wave of the sea, but solid and eternal, rolling away to the infinite distance, but sheltering in its folds quiet villages whose smoke rises in frail columns by day, whose lamps burn in the immense darkness by night. Gabriel Oak tending his sheep up there on the back of the world is the eternal shepherd; the stars are ancient beacons; and for ages he has watched beside his sheep.

But down in the valley the earth is full of warmth and life; the farms are busy, the barns stored, the fields loud with the lowing of cattle and the bleating of sheep. Nature is prolific, splendid and lustful; not yet malignant and still the Great Mother of labouring men. And now for the first time Hardy gives full play to his humour, where it is freest and most rich, upon the lips of country men. Jan Coggan and Henry Fray and Joseph Poorgrass gather in the malthouse when the day's work is over and give vent to that half-shrewd, half-poetic humour which has been brewing in their brains and finding expression over their beer since the pilgrims tramped the Pilgrims' Way; which Shakespeare and Scott and George Eliot all loved to over-hear, but none loved better or heard with greater under-standing than Hardy. But it is not the part of the peasants in the Wessex novels to stand out as individuals. They compose a pool of common wisdom, a fund of perpetual life. They comment upon the actions of the hero and heroine, but while Troy or Oak or Fanny or Bathsheba come in and out and pass away, Jan Coggan and Henry Fray and Joseph Poorgrass remain. They drink by night and they plough the fields by day. They are eternal. We meet them over and over again in the novels, and they always have something typical about them, more of the character that marks a race than of the features which belong to an individual. The peasants are the great sanctuary of sanity, the country the last stronghold of happiness. When they disappear, there is no hope for the race.

With Oak and Troy and Bathsheba and Fanny Robin we come to the men and women of the novels at their full stature. In every book three or four figures predominate, and stand up like lightning conductors to attract the force of the elements. Oak and Troy and Bathsheba; Eustacia, Wildeve and Venn; Henchard, Lucetta and Farfrae; Jude, Sue Bridehead and Phillotson. There is even a certain likeness between the different groups. They live as individuals and they differ as individuals; but they also live as types and have a likeness as types. Bathsheba is Bathsheba, but she is woman and sister to Eustacia and Lucetta and Sue; Gabriel Oak is Gabriel Oak, but he is man and brother to Henchard, Venn and Jude. However lovable and charming Bathsheba may be, still she is weak; however stubborn and ill-guided Henchard may be, still he is strong. This is fundamental; this is the core of Hardy's vision, and drawn from the deepest sources of his nature. The woman is the weaker and the fleshlier, and she clings to the stronger and obscures his vision. How freely, nevertheless, in his greater books life is poured over the unalterable framework! When Bathsheba sits in the wagon among her plants, smiling at her own loveliness in the little looking-glass, we may know, and it is proof of Hardy's power that we do know, how severely she will suffer and cause others to suffer before the end. But the moment has all the bloom and beauty of life. And so it is, time and time again. His characters, both men and women, were creatures to him of an infinite attraction. For the women he shows a more tender solicitude than for the men, and in them, perhaps, he takes a keener interest. Vain might their beauty be and terrible their fate, but while the glow of life is in them their step is free, their laughter sweet, and theirs is the power to sink into the breast of nature and become part of her silence and solemnity, or to rise and put on them the movement of the clouds and the wildness of the flowering woodlands. The men who suffer, not like the women through dependence upon other human beings, but through conflict with fate, enlist our sterner sympathies. For such a man as Gabriel Oak we need have no passing fears. Honour him we must, though it is not granted us to love him quite so freely. He is firmly set upon his feet and can give as shrewd a blow, to men at least, as any he is likely to receive. He has a prevision of what is to be expected that springs from character rather than from education. He is stable in his temperament, steadfast in his affections, and capable of open-eyed endurance without flinching. But he, too, is no puppet. He is a homely, humdrum fellow on ordinary occasions. He can walk the street without making people turn to stare at him. In short, nobody can deny Hardy's power – the true novelist's power – to make us believe that his characters are fellow-beings driven by their own passions and idiosyncrasies, while they have – and this is the poet's gift – something symbolical about them which is common to us all.

And it is at this point, when we are considering Hardy's power of creating men and women, that we become most conscious of the profound differences that distinguish him from his peers. We look back at a number of these characters and ask ourselves what it is that we remember them for. We recall their passions. We remember how deeply they have loved each other and often with what tragic results. We remember the faithful love of Oak for Bathsheba; the tumultuous but fleeting passions of men like Wildeve, Troy and Fitzspiers; we remember the filial love of Clym for his mother, the jealous paternal passion of Henchard for Elizabeth Jane. But we do not remember how they have loved. We do not remember how they talked and changed and got to know each other, finely, gradually, from step to step and from stage to stage. Their relationship is not composed of those intellectual apprehensions and subtleties of perception which seem so slight yet are so profound. In all the books love is one of the great facts that mould human life. But it is a catastrophe; it happens suddenly and overwhelmingly, and there is little to be said about it. The talk between the lovers when it is not passionate is practical or philosophic, as though the discharge of their daily duties left them with more desire to question life and its purpose than to investigate each other's sensibilities. Even if it were in their characters to analyse their emotions, life is too stirring to give them time. They need all their strength to deal with the downright blows, the freakish ingenuity, the gradually increasing malignity of fate. They have none to spend upon the subtleties and delicacies of the human comedy.

Thus there comes a time when we can say with certainty that we shall not find in Hardy some of the qualities that have given us most delight in the works of other novelists. He has not the perfection of Jane Austen, or the wit of Meredith, or the range of Thackeray, or Tolstoy's amazing intellectual power. There is in the work of the great classical writers a finality of effect which places certain of their scenes, apart from the story, beyond the reach of change. We do not ask what bearing they have upon the narrative, nor do we make use of them to interpret problems which lie on the outskirts of the scene. A laugh, a blush, half a dozen words of dialogue, and it is enough; the source of our delight is perennial. But Hardy has none of this concentration and completeness. His light does not fall directly upon the human heart. It passes over it and out on to the darkness of the heath and upon the trees swaying in the storm. When we look back into the room the group by the fireside is dispersed. Each man or woman is battling with the storm, alone, revealing himself most when he is least under the observation of other human beings. We do not know them as we know Pierre or Natasha or Becky Sharp. We do not know them in and out and all round as they are revealed to the casual caller, to the Government official, to the great lady, to the general on the battlefield. We do not know the complication and involvement and turmoil of their thoughts. Geographically, too, they remain fixed to the same stretch of the English countryside, and it is seldom, and not with happy results, that Hardy leaves the yeoman or farmer to describe the class above theirs in the social scale. In the drawing-room and clubroom and ballroom, where people of leisure and education come together, where comedy is bred and shades of character revealed, he is awkward and ill at ease. But the opposite is equally true. If we do not know his men and women in their relations to each other, we know them in their relations to time, death and fate. If we do not see them in quick agitation against the lights and crowds of cities, we see them against the earth, the storm and the seasons. We know their attitude towards some of the most tremendous problems that can confront mankind. They take on a more than mortal size in memory. We see them not in detail but enlarged and dignified. We see Tess reading the baptismal service in her nightgown 'with an impress of dignity that was almost regal'. We see Marty South, 'like a being who had rejected with indifference the attribute of sex for the loftier quality of abstract human-ism', laying the flowers on Winterbourne's grave. Their speech has a Biblical dignity and poetry. They have a force in them which cannot be defined, a force of love or of hate, a force which in the men is the cause of rebellion against life, and in the women implies an illimitable capacity for suffering, and it is this which dominates the character and makes it unnecessary that we should see the finer features that lie hid. This is the tragic power; and, if we are to place Hardy among his fellows, we must call him the greatest tragic writer among English novel-ists. Thus, if we are to appreciate him truly we must look at the outer conflict, not at the inner; we must read him for his scenes, not for his sentences; for his poetry, not for his prose.

But let us, as we approach the danger-zone of Hardy's philosophy, be on our guard. Nothing is more necessary, in reading an imaginative writer, than to keep at the right distance above his page. Nothing is easier, especially with a writer of marked tendency, than to fasten on opinions, convict him of a creed, tether him to a consistent point of view. Nor was Hardy any exception to the rule that the mind which is most capable of receiving impressions is very often the least capable of drawing conclusions. It is for the reader, steeped in the impression, to supply the comment. It is his part to know when to put aside the writer's conscious intention in favour of some deeper intention of which perhaps he may be unconscious. Hardy himself was aware of this. A novel 'is an impression, not an argument', he has warned us, and, again: 'Unadjusted impressions have their value, and the road to a true philosophy of life seems to lie in humbly recording diverse readings of its phenomena as they are forced upon us by chance and change'. Certainly it is true to say of him that at his greatest, he gives us impressions; at his weakest, arguments. In *The Woodlanders*, *The Return of the Native*, *Far from the Madding Crowd*, and, above all, in *The Mayor of Casterbridge*, we have Hardy's impression of life as it came to him without conscious ordering. Let him once begin to tamper with his direct intuitions and his power is gone. 'Did you say the stars were worlds, Tess?' asks little Abraham as they drive to market with their beehives. Tess replies that they are like 'the apples on our stubbard-tree, most of them splendid and sound – a few blighted'. 'Which do we live on – a splendid or a blighted one?' 'A blighted one', she replies, or rather the mournful thinker who has assumed her mask speaks for her. The words protrude, cold and raw, like the springs of a machine where we had seen only flesh and blood. We are crudely jolted out of that mood of sympathy which is renewed a moment later when the little cart is run down and we have a concrete instance of the ironical methods which rule our planet.

That is the reason why *Jude the Obscure* is the most painful of all Hardy's books, and the only one against which we can fairly bring the charge of pessimism. In *Jude the Obscure* argument is allowed to dominate impression, with the result that though the misery of the book is overwhelming it is not tragic. As calamity succeeds calamity we feel that the case against society is not being argued fairly or with profound understanding of the facts. Here is nothing of that width and force and knowledge of mankind which, when Tolstoy criticizes society, makes his indictment formidable. Here we have revealed to us the petty cruelty of men, not the large injustice of the gods. It is only necessary to compare *Jude the Obscure* with *The Mayor of Casterbridge* to see where Hardy's true power lay. Jude carries on his miserable contest against the deans of colleges and the conventions of sophisticated society. Henchard is pitted, not against another man, but against something outside himself which is opposed to men of his ambition and power. No human being wishes him ill. Even Farfrae and Newson and Elizabeth Jane whom he has wronged all come to pity him, and even to admire his strength of character. He is standing up to fate, and in backing the old Mayor whose ruin has been largely his own fault, Hardy makes us feel that we are backing human nature in an unequal contest. There is no pessimism here. Throughout the book we are aware of the sublimity of the issue, and yet it is presented to us in the most concrete form. From the opening scene in which Henchard sells his wife to the sailor at the fair to his death on Egdon Heath the vigour of the story is superb, its humour rich and racy, its movement large-limbed and free. The skimmity ride, the fight between Farfrae and Henchard in the loft, Mrs. Cuxsom's speech upon the death of Mrs. Henchard, the talk of the ruffians at Peter's Finger with nature present in the background or mysteriously dominating the foreground, are among the glories of English fiction. Meagre and scanty, it may be, is the measure of happiness allowed to each, but so long as the struggle is as Henchard's was, with the decrees of fate and not with the laws of man, so long as it is in the open air and calls for activity of the body rather than of the brain, there is greatness in the contest, and the death of the broken corn merchant in his cottage on Egdon Heath is comparable to the death of Ajax lord of Salamis. The true tragic emotion is ours.

Before such power as this we are made to feel that the ordinary tests which we apply to fiction are futile enough. Do we insist that a great novelist shall be a master of melodious prose? Hardy was no such thing. He feels his way by dint of sagacity and uncompromising sincerity to the phrase he wants, and it is often of unforgettable pungency. Failing it, he will make do with any homely or clumsy or old-fashioned turn of speech, now of the utmost plainness, now of a bookish elaboration. No style in literature, save Scott's, is so difficult to analyse; it is on the face of it so bad, yet it achieves its aim so unmistakably. As well might one attempt to rationalize the charm of a muddy country road, or of a plain field of roots in winter. And then like Dorsetshire itself, out of these very elements of stiffness and angularity his prose will put on greatness; will roll with a Latin sonority; will shape itself in a massive and monumental symmetry like that of his own bare downs. Then again, do we require that a novelist shall observe the probabilities, and keep close to reality? To find anything approaching the violence and convolution of Hardy's plots one must go back to the Elizabethan drama. Yet we accept his story completely as we read it; and more than that, it becomes obvious that his violence and his melodrama, when they are not due to a curious peasantlike love of the monstrous for its own sake, are part of that wild spirit of poetry which saw with intense irony and grimness that no reading of life can possibly outdo the strangeness of life itself, no symbol of caprice and unreason be too extreme to represent the astonishing circumstances of our existence.

But as we consider the great structure of the Wessex novels it seems irrelevant to fasten on little points – this character, that scene, this phrase of deep and poetic beauty. It is something larger that Hardy has bequeathed to us. Like every great novelist, he gives us not merely a world which we can liken to the world we know, but an attitude towards it, an atmosphere surrounding it, which is of far greater importance and lasts long after the world which the novelist portrays has vanished for ever. This spirit, though it is in the scene, exists apart from the scene. It is in the life and character of the writer, as well as in the art and language that he uses. The greater the writer, the more completely the different elements are fused into one. That is why the effect of a great novel is so commanding, so complete, and yet so extremely difficult to analyse in words. When we read the Wessex novels we have to free ourselves from the cramp and pettiness imposed by life. Our imaginations have to expand and soar; our humour has to laugh out; we have to drink deep of the beauty of the earth. But also we have to enter the shade of a sorrowful and brooding spirit which even in its saddest mood still bore itself with a grave uprightness and never, even when most moved to anger, lost its simple tenderness for the sufferings of men and women. Thus it is no mere transcript of life at a certain time and place that Hardy has given us. It is a vision of the world and of man's lot as they revealed themselves to an astonishing imagination, a profound and poetic genius, a gentle and humane soul. It is for this, a gift of lasting and inexhaustible value, that we have to thank him today.

Fanny Burney's Half-Sister

Since a copy of *Evelina* was lately sold for the enormous sum of four thousand pounds; since the Clarendon Press has lately bestowed the magnificent compliment of a new edition upon *Evelina*; since Maria Allen was the half-sister of the authoress of *Evelina*; since the story of Evelina owed much to the story of Maria Allen, it may not be impertinent to consider what is still to be collected of the history of that misguided and unfortunate girl.

As is well known, Dr. Burney was twice married. He took for his second wife a Mrs. Allen of Lynn, the widow of a substantial citizen who left her with a fortune which she promptly lost, and with three children, of whom one, Maria, was almost the same age as Fanny Burney when Dr. Burney's second marriage made them half-sisters. And half-sisters they might have remained with none but a formal tie between them, had not the differences between the two families brought about a much closer relationship. The Burneys were the gifted children of gifted parents. They had enjoyed all the stimulus that comes from running in and out of rooms where grown-up people are talking about books and music, where the piano is always open, and somebody – it may be David Garrick, it may be Mrs. Thrale – is always dropping in to dinner. Maria, on the other hand, had been bred in the provinces. The great figures of Lynn were well known to her, but the great figures of Lynn were merely Miss Dolly Young – who was so ugly – or Mr. Richard Warren, who was so handsome. The talk she heard was the talk of squires and merchants. Her greatest excitement was a dance at the Assembly Rooms or a scandal in the town.

Thus she was rustic and unsophisticated where the Burneys were metropolitan and cultivated. But she was bold and dashing where they were timid and reserved. She was all agog for life and adventure where they were always running away in agonies of shyness to commit their innumerable observations to reams of paper. Unrefined, but generous and unaffected, she brought to Poland-street that whiff of fresh air that contact with ordinary life and ease in the presence of ordinary things, which the precocious family lacked themselves and found most refreshing in others. Sometimes she visited them in London; sometimes they stayed with her at Lynn. Soon she came to feel for them all, but for Fanny in particular, a warm, a genuine, a surprised admiration. They were so learned and so innocent; they knew so many things, and yet they did not know half as much about life as she did. It was to them, naturally, that she confided her own peccadilloes and adventures, wishing perhaps for counsel, wishing perhaps to impress. Fanny was one of those shy people – 'I am not near so squeamish as you are', Maria observed – who draw out the confidences of their bolder friends and delight in accounts of actions which they could not possibly commit themselves. Thus in 1770 Fanny was imparting to her diary certain confidences that Maria had made her of such a nature that when she read the book later she judged it best to tear out twelve pages and burn them. Happily, a packet of letters survives which, though rather meagrely doled out by an editor in the eighties, who thought them too full of dashes to be worthy of the dignity of print, allow us to guess pretty clearly what kind of secret Maria confided and Fanny recorded, and Fanny, grown mature, then tore up.

For example, there was an Assembly at Lynn some time in 1770 to which Maria did not want to go. Bet Dickens, however, overcame her scruples, and she went. However, she was determined not to dance. However, she did dance. Martin was there. She broke her earring. She danced a minuet à quatre. She got into the chariot to come home. She came home. 'Was I alone? – guess – well, all is vanity and vexations of spirit.' It needs little ingenuity to interpret these nods and winks and innuendoes. Maria danced with Martin. She came home with

Martin. She sat alone with Martin, and she had been strictly forbidden by her mother to meet Martin. That is obvious. But what is not, after all these years, quite too clear is for what reason Mrs. Allen disapproved. On the face of it Martin Rishton was a very good match for Maria Allen. He was well born, he had been educated at Oxford, he was the heir of his uncle Sir Richard Bettenson, and Sir Richard Bettenson had five thousand a year and no children. Nevertheless, Maria's mother warmly opposed the match. She said rather vaguely that Martin 'had been extravagant at Oxford, and that she had heard some story that he had done something unworthy of a gentleman'. But her ostensible objections were based perhaps upon others which were less easy to state. There was her daughter's character for example. Maria was 'a droll girl with a very great love of sport and mirth'. Her temper was lively and warm. She was extremely outspoken. 'If possible', Fanny said, 'she is too sincere. She pays too little regard to the world; and indulges herself with too much freedom of raillery and pride of disdain towards those whose vices and follies offend her.' When Mrs. Allen looked from Maria to Martin she saw, there can be no doubt, something that made her uneasy. But what? Perhaps it was nothing more than that Martin was particular about appearances and Maria rather slack; that Martin was conventional by nature and Maria the very opposite; that Martin liked dress and decorum and that

Maria was one of those heedless girls who say the first thing that comes into their heads and never reflect, if they are amused themselves, what people will say if they have holes in their stockings. Whatever the reason, Mrs. Allen forbade the match; and Sir Richard Bettenson, whether to meet her views or for educational purposes, sent his nephew in the beginning of 1771 to travel for two years abroad. Maria remained at Lynn.

Five months, however, had not passed before Martin burst in unexpectedly at a dinner-party of relations in Welbeck-street. He looked very well, but when he was asked why he had come back in such a hurry, 'he smiled, but said nothing to the question'. Maria, although still at Lynn, at once got wind of his arrival. Soon she saw him at a dance, but she did not dance with him and the ban was evidently enforced, for her letters become plaintive and agitated and hint at secrets that she cannot reveal, even to her dear toads the Burneys. It was now her turn to be sent abroad, partly to be out of Martin's way, partly to finish her education. She was dispatched to Geneva. But the Burneys soon received a packet from her. In the first place, she had some little commissions that she must ask them to discharge. Would they send her a pianoforte, some music, Fordyce's sermons, a tea cadet, an ebony inkstand with silver-plated tops, and a very pretty naked wax doll with blue eyes to be had in Fleet-street for half-a-crown – all of which, if well wrapped up, could travel safely in the case of the pianoforte. She had no money to pay with at the moment, for she had been persuaded and indeed was sure that it was true economy if one passed through Paris to spend all one's money on clothes. But she could always sell her diamonds or she would give them 'a bill on somebody in London'. These trifling matters dispatched, she turned to something of far greater importance. Indeed, what she had to say was so important that it must be burnt at once. Indeed, it was only her great distress and being alone in a foreign land that led her to tell them at all. But the truth was – so far as can now be ascertained among the fragments and the dashes – the truth was that she had gone much farther with Martin than anybody knew. She had in fact confessed her love to him. And he had proposed something which had made her very angry. She had refused to do it. She had written him a very angry letter. She had had indeed to write it three times over before she got it right. When he read it he was furious. 'Did my character', he wrote, 'ever give you reason to imagine I should expose you because you loved me? 'Tis thoroughly unnatural – I defy the world to bring an instance of my behaving unworthy the Character of a Gentleman.' These were his very words. And, Maria wrote, 'I think such the sentiments of a Man of Honour, and such I hope to find him', she concluded; for although she knew very well that Hetty Burney and Mr. Crisp disliked him, he was – here she came out with it – the man 'on whom all my happiness in this Life depends and in whom I *wish* to see no faults'. The Burneys hid the letters, breathed not a word to their parents, and waited in suspense. Nor did they have to wait long. Before the spring was over Maria was back again in Poland-street and in circumstances so romantic, so exciting, and above all so secret that 'I dare not', Fanny exclaimed, 'commit particulars to paper'. This much (and one would have thought it enough) only could be said. 'Miss Allen – for the last time I shall call her so – came home on Monday last ... she was married last Saturday!' It was true. Martin Rishton had gone out secretly to join her abroad. They had been married at Ypres on May 16 1772. On the 18th Maria reached England and confided the grand secret to Fanny and Susan Burney, but she told no one else. They were afraid to tell her mother. They were afraid to tell Dr. Burney. In their dilemma they turned to the strange man who was always their confidant – to Samuel Crisp of Chessington.

Many years before this Samuel Crisp had retired from the world. He had been a man of parts, a man of fashion and a man of great social charm. But his fine friends had wasted his substance and his clever friends had damned his play. In disgust with the insincerity of fashionable life and the fickleness of fame he had withdrawn to a decayed manor house near London, which, however, was so far from the high road and so hidden from travellers in the waste of a common that no one could find it unless specially instructed. But Mr. Crisp was careful to issue no instructions. The Burneys were almost the only friends who knew the way across the fields to his door. But the Burneys could never come often enough. He depended upon the Burneys for life and society and for news of the great world which he despised and yet could not forget. The Burney children stood to him in the place of his own children. Upon them he lavished all the shrewdness and knowledge and disillusionment which he had won at such cost to himself and now found so useless in an old manor house on a wild common with only old Mrs. Hamilton and young Kitty Cook to bear him company.

It was then to Chessington and to Daddy Crisp that Maria Rishton and Susan Burney made their way on June 7 with their tremendous secret burning in their breasts. At first Maria was too nervous to tell him the plain truth. She tried to enlighten him with hints and hums and haws. But she succeeded only in rousing his wrath against Martin, which he expressed so strongly, 'almost calling him a Mahoon', that Maria began to kindle and ran off in a huff to her bedroom. Here she resolved to take the bull by the horns. She summoned Kitty Cook and sent her to Mr. Crisp with a saucy message: 'Mrs Rishton sent compts, and hoped to see him at Stanhoe this summer'. Upon receiving the message Mr. Crisp came in haste to the girls' bedroom. An extraordinary scene then took place. Maria knelt on the floor and hid her face in the bedclothes. Mr. Crisp commanded her to tell the truth – was she indeed Mrs. Rishton? Maria could not speak. Kitty Cook 'claw'd hold of her left hand and shew'd him the ring'. Then Susan produced two letters from Martin which proved the fact beyond doubt. They had been married legally. They were man and wife. If that were so, there was only one thing to be done, Mr. Crisp declared – Mrs. Burney must be informed and the marriage must be made public at once. He behaved with all the sense and decision of a man of the world. He wrote to Maria's mother; he explained the whole situation. On getting the letter Mrs. Burney was extremely angry. She received the couple – she could do nothing else – but she never liked Martin and she never altogether forgave her daughter. However, the deed was done, and now the young couple had nothing to do but to settle down to enjoy the delights which they had snatched so impetuously.

All now depended, for those who loved Maria – and Fanny Burney loved her very dearly – upon the character of Martin Rishton. Was he, as Mr. Crisp almost said, a Mahoon? Or was he, as his sister openly declared, a Bashaw? Would he make her happy or would he not? The discerning and affectionate eyes of Fanny were now turned observingly upon Martin to find out. And yet it was very difficult to find out anything for certain. He was a strange mixture. He was high-spirited; he was 'prodigiously agreeable'. But he was somehow, with his talk of vulgarity and distinction, rather exacting – he liked his wife to do him credit. For example, the Rishtons went on to take the waters at Bath, and there were the usual gaieties in progress. Fischer was giving a concert, and the eldest Miss Linley was singing, perhaps for the last time. All Bath would be there. But poor Maria sat alone in the lodgings writing to Fanny, and the reason she gave was a strange one. Martin, 'who is rather more exact about dress than I am, can't think of my appearing' unless she bought a 'suit of mignionet linen fringed for second mourning' to go in. She refused; the dress was too expensive; 'and as he was unwilling I should appear else, I gave up the dear Fischer – see what a cruel thing to have a sposo who is rather a p-p-y in those sort of things'. So there she sat alone; and she hated Bath; and she found servants such a nuisance – she had had to dismiss the butler already. At the same time, she was head over heels in love with her Rishy, and one would like to suppose that the tiff about the dress was made up by the present of Romeo, the remarkably fine brown Pomeranian dog, which Martin bought for a large sum at this time and gave her. Martin himself had a passion for dogs.

It was no doubt in order to gratify his love of sport and Maria's dislike of towns that they moved on later that spring to Teignmouth, or as Maria calls it to 'Tingmouth', in Devon. The move was entirely to her liking. Her letters gushed and burbled, had fewer stops and more dashes than ever, as she endeavoured to describe the delights of Tingmouth to Fanny in London. Their cottage was 'one of the neatest Thatch'd cottages you ever saw'. It belonged to a sea captain. It was full of china glass flowers that he had brought home from his voyages. It was hung with prints from the Prayer-book and the Bible. There were also two pictures, one said to be by Raphael, the other by Correggio. The Miss Minifies might have described it as a retreat for a heroine. It looked on to a green. The fisher people were simple and happy. Their cottages were clean and their children were healthy. The sea was full of whiting, salmon and young mackerel. Martin had bought a brace of beautiful spaniels. It was a great diversion to make them go into the water. 'Indeed, we intend getting a very large Newfoundland dog before we leave this place.' And they intended to go for expeditions and take their dinner with them. And Fanny must come. Nothing could serve them but that Fanny should come and stay. It was monstrous for her to say that she must stop at home and copy her father's manuscripts. She must come at once; and if she came she need not spend a penny, for Maria wore nothing but a common linen gown and had not had her hair dressed once since she came here. In short, Fanny must come.

Thus solicited, Fanny arrived some time in July, 1773, and for almost two months lodged in the boxroom – the other rooms were so littered with dogs and poultry that they had to put her in the boxroom – and observed the humours of Tingmouth society and the moods of the lovers. There could be no doubt that they were still very much in love, but the truth was that Tingmouth was very gay. A great many families made it their summer resort; there were the Phippses and the Hurrels and the Westerns and the Colbournes; there was Mr. Crispen – perhaps the most distinguished man in Tingmouth – Mr. Green who lodged with Mr. Crispen and Miss Bowdler. Naturally, in so small a place, everybody knew everybody. The Phippses, the Hurrels, the Rishtons, the Colbournes, Mr. Crispen, Mr. Green and Miss Bowdler must meet incessantly. They must make up parties to go to the wrestling matches, and attend the races in their whiskeys, and see the country people run after a pig whose tail had been cut off. Much coming and going was inevitable; but, as Fanny soon observed, it was not altogether to Martin's liking. 'They will soon make this as errant a public place as Bristol Hot wells or any other place', he grumbled. He had nothing whatever to say against the Phippses or the Westerns; he had the greatest respect for the Hurrels, which was odd, considering how very fat and greedy Mr. Hurrel was; Mr. Crispen, of course, who lived at Bath and spoke Italian perfectly, one must respect; but the fact was, Martin confided to Fanny, that he 'almost detested' Miss Bowdler. Miss Bowdler came of a respectable family.

Her brother was destined to edit Shakespeare. Her family were old friends of the Allens. One could not forbid her the house; in fact she was always in and out of it; and yet, said Martin, 'he could not endure even the sight of her'. 'A woman', said Martin, 'who despises the customs and manners of the country she lives in, must, consequently, conduct herself with impropriety.' And, indeed, she did. For though she was only twenty-six she had come to Tingmouth alone; and then she made no secret of the fact, indeed she avowed it quite openly, 'in the fair face of day', that she visited Mr. Crispen in his lodgings, and not merely paid a call but stayed to supper. Nobody had 'the most distant shadow of doubt of Miss Bowdler's being equally innocent with those who have more worldly prudence', but at the same time nobody could doubt that Miss Bowdler found the society of gentlemen more enter-taining than that of ladies – or could deny that though Mr. Crispen was old, Mr. Green who lodged with him was young. Then, of course, she came on to the Rishtons and encouraged Maria in her least desirable attribute – her levity, her love of chaff, her carelessness of dress and deportment. It was deplorable.

Fanny Burney liked Martin very much and listened to his complaints with sympathy; but for all her charm and distinction, indeed because of them, she was destined unfortunately to make matters worse. Among her gifts she had the art of being extremely attractive to elderly gentlemen. Soon Mr. Crispen was paying her outrageous attentions. 'Little Burney', he said, was irresistible; the name of Burney would be found – with many others, Miss Bowdler interjected – cut upon his heart. Mr. Crispen must implore one kiss. It was said of course in jest, but Miss Bowdler took it of course in earnest. Had she not nursed Mr. Crispen through a dangerous illness? Had she not sacrificed her maidenly reputation by visiting him in his cottage? And then Martin, who had been perhaps already annoyed by Mr. Crispen's social predominance, found it galling in the extreme to have that gentleman always in the house, always paying outrageous compliments to his guest. Anything that 'led towards flirtation' he disliked; and soon Mr. Crispen had become, Fanny observed, almost as odious as Miss Bowdler. He threw himself into the study of the Italian grammar; he read aloud to Maria and Fanny from the *Faery Queen*, 'omitting whatever, to the poet's great disgrace, has crept in that is improper for a woman's ear'. But what with Miss Bowdler, Mr. Crispen, the Tingmothians and the influence of undesirable acquaintances upon his wife, there can be no doubt that Martin was very uncomfortable at Tingmouth, and when the time came, September 17, to say good-bye he appeared 'in monstrous spirits'. Perhaps everybody was glad that the summer was at an end. They were glad to say good-bye and glad to be able to say it in civil terms. Mr. Crispen left for Bath; and Miss

Bowdler – there is no rashness in the assumption – left, for Bath also.

The Rishtons proceeded in their whiskey with all their dogs left to visit the Westerns, one of the few families with whom Martin cared to associate. But the journey was unfortunate. They began by taking the wrong turning, then they ran over Tingmouth, the Newfoundland dog, who was running under the body of the whiskey. Then at Oxford Maria longed to see the colleges, but feeling sure that Martin's pride would be hurt at showing himself in a whiskey with a wife where in the old days he had 'shone forth a gay bachelor with a phaeton and four bays', she refused his offer to take her, and had her hair dressed, very badly, instead. Off they went again, and again they ran over two more dogs. Worst of all, when they arrived at the Westerns', they found the whole house shut up and the Westerns gone to Buckinghamshire. Altogether it was an unfortunate expedition. And it is impossible, as one reads Maria's breathless volubility to Fanny, to resist the conviction that the journey with its accidents and mistakes, with its troop of dogs, and Martin's pride, and Maria's fears and her recourse to the hairdresser and the hairdresser's ill success, and Martin's memories of gay bachelor days and phaetons and bay horses and his respect for the Westerns and his love of servants was typical of the obscure years of married life that were now to succeed each other at Stanhoe, in Norfolk.

At Stanhoe they lived the lives of country gentry. They repaired the ancient house, though they had but the lease of it. They planted and cleaned and cut new walks in the garden. They bought a cow and started a dairy for Maria. Dog was added to dog – rare dogs, wonderful dogs, spaniels, lurchers, Portugal pointers from the banks of the Dowrow. To keep up the establishment as establishments should be kept up, nine servants, in Martin's opinion, were none too many. And so, though she had no children, Maria found that all her time was occupied with her household and the care of her establishment. But how far better, she wrote, to be active like this instead of leading 'the loitering life' she had led at Tingmouth! Surely, Maria continued, scribbling her heart out ungrammatically to Fanny Burney, 'there are pleasures for every station and employment', and one cannot be bored if 'as I hope I am acting properly'; so that in sober truth she did not envy Fanny Lord Stanhope's *fête champêtre*, since she had her chickens and her dairy, and Tingmouth, who had had the distemper, must be led out on a string. Why, then, regret Miss Bowdler and Mr. Crispen and the sport and gaiety of the old days at Tingmouth? Nevertheless, the old days kept coming back to her mind. At Tingmouth, she reflected, they had only kept a man and a maid. Here they had nine servants, and the more there are the more 'cabally and insolent' they become. And then relations came over from Lynn and pried into her kitchen and made her more 'bashful', as Martin would say, than ever. And then if she sat down to her tambour for half an hour Martin, 'who is I believe the Most Active Creature alive', would burst in and say, 'Come Maria, you must go with me and see how charmingly Damon hunts' – or he would say 'I know of a pheasant's nest about two miles off, you shall go and see it'.

> Then away we trail broiling over Cornfields – and when we come to the pit some Unlucky boy has Stole the Eggs ... then I spend Whole Mornings seeing him Shoot Rooks – grub up trees – and at night for we never come in now till Nine o'clock – when tea is over and I have settled my accounts or done some company business – bed-time Comes.

Bedtime had come; and the day had been somehow disappointing.

How could she mend matters? How could she save money so that Martin could buy the phaeton upon which his heart had been set ever since they were married? She might save on dress, for she did not mind what she wore; but alas! Martin was very particular still; he did not like her to dress in linen. So she must manage better in the house, and she was not formed to manage servants. Thus she began to dwell upon those happy days before she had gone to Tingmouth, before she had married, before she had nine servants and a phaeton and ever so many dogs. She began to brood over that still more distant time when she had first known the Burneys and they had sat 'browsing over my little [fire] and eating good things out of the closet by the fire side'. Her thoughts turned to all those friends whom she had lost, to that 'lovd society which I remember with the greatest pleasure'; and she could never forget in particular the paternal kindness of Dr. Burney. Oh, she sighed as she sat alone in Norfolk among the pheasants and the fields, how she wished that 'none of my family had ever quitted his sheltering roof till placed under the protection of a worthy husband'. For her own marriage – but enough; they had been very much in love; they had been very happy; she must go and do her hair; she must try to please her Rishy. And so the obscure history of the Rishtons fades away, save what is preserved by the sprightly pen of Maria's half-sister in the pages of *Evelina*. And yet – the reflection will occur – if Fanny had seen more of Maria and more of Mr. Crispen and even more of Miss Bowdler and the Tingmouth set, her later books, had they been less refined, might have been as amusing as her first.

Aurora Leigh

By one of those ironies of fashion that might have amused
the Brownings themselves, it seems likely that they are
now far better known in the flesh than they have ever
been in the spirit. Passionate lovers, in curls and side
whiskers, oppressed, defiant, eloping – in this guise
thousands of people must know and love the Brownings
who have never read a line of their poetry. They have
become two of the most conspicuous figures in the bright
and animated procession which, thanks to our modern
habit of printing letters and writing memoirs and sitting
to be photographed, keeps step with the paler, subtler,
more obscure shades who, in times gone by, lived solely
between the pages of their books. To such immortality
the Brownings, of course, laid themselves peculiarly
open. Their story appeals to all that is dramatic and
romantic in our natures. He must be dull, blind and no
better than a bookworm who does not unravel the story
of their hearts with enthusiasm and pore with delight
over the picture of tiny Miss Barrett issuing one September

morning from the dark house in Wimpole-street with Flush under her arm and the maid Wilson following behind to meet Browning, Italy, health and freedom in the church round the corner.

But it cannot be denied that the works of the Brownings have lost lustre even as much as their persons have gained it. 'Sordello', *The Ring and the Book*, *Men and Women* and the rest are said to have little significance and little resonance in modern ears. Is it worth while, people ask, to sort this tangle of untidy verbiage in order to find the rather dubious treasures of a hearty, cheerful middle-class mind concealed beneath? As for Elizabeth Barrett Browning, her fate as a writer is far worse than her husband's. Nobody reads her, nobody discusses her poems, nobody troubles to put her in her place. One has only to compare her reputation with Christina Rossetti's to trace her decline. Christina Rossetti mounts irresistibly to the first place among English women poets. Elizabeth, so much more loudly applauded during her lifetime, falls farther and farther behind. The primers dismiss her with contumely. Her importance, they say, 'has now become merely historical. Neither education nor association with her husband ever succeeded in teaching her the value of words and a sense of form.' In short, the only place in the mansion of literature that is assigned her is downstairs in the servants' quarters, where, in company with Mrs. Hemans, Eliza Cook, Jean Ingelow, Alexander Smith,

Edwin Arnold and Robert Montgomery she bangs the crockery about and eats vast handfuls of peas on the point of her knife.

If, therefore, we take *Aurora Leigh* from the shelf it is not so much in order to read it as to muse with kindly condescension over this token of bygone fashion, as we toy with the fringes of our grandmothers' mantles and muse over alabaster models of the Taj Mahal which once adorned their drawing-room tables. But to the Victorians, undoubtedly, the book was very dear. Thirteen editions of *Aurora Leigh* had been demanded by the year 1873. And, to judge from the dedication, Mrs. Browning herself was not afraid to say that she set great store by it – 'the most mature of my works', she calls it, 'and the one into which my highest convictions upon Life and Art have entered'. Her letters show that she had had the book in mind for many years. She was brooding over it when she first met Browning, and her intention with regard to it forms almost the first of those confidences about their work which the lovers delighted to share. '... my chief *intention*', she wrote, 'just now is the writing of a sort of novel-poem ... running into the midst of our conventions, and rushing into drawing rooms and the like, "where angels fear to tread"; and so, meeting face to face and without mask the Humanity of the age, and speaking the truth of it out plainly. That is my intention.' But for reasons which later become clear, she hoarded her intention throughout the ten astonishing years of escape and happiness; and when at last the book appeared in 1856 she might well feel that she had poured into it the best that she had to give. Perhaps the hoarding and the saturation which resulted have something to do with the surprise that awaits us. At any rate we cannot read the first twenty pages of *Aurora Leigh* without becoming aware that the Ancient Mariner who lingers, for unknown reasons, at the porch of one book and not of another has us by the hand, and makes us listen like a three years child while Mrs. Browning pours out in nine volumes of blank verse the story of Aurora Leigh. Speed and energy, forthrightness and complete self-confidence – these are the qualities that hold us enthralled. Floated off our feet by them we learn how Aurora was the child of an Italian mother 'whose rare blue eyes were shut from seeing her when she was scarcely four years old'. Her father was 'an austere Englishman, Who, after a dry life-time spent at home In college-learning, law and parish talk, Was flooded with a passion unaware', but died, too, and the child was sent back to England to be brought up by an aunt. The aunt, of the well-known family of the Leighs, stood upon the hall step of her country house dressed in black to welcome her. Her somewhat narrow forehead was braided tight with brown hair pricked with grey; she had a close, mild mouth; eyes of no colour; and cheeks like roses pressed in books, 'Kept more for ruth than pleasure, – if past bloom, Past fading also'. The lady had lived a quiet life, exercising her Christian gifts upon knitting stockings, and stitching petticoats 'because we are of one flesh, after all, and need one flannel'. At her hand Aurora suffered the education that was thought proper for women. She learnt a little French, a little algebra; the internal laws of the Burmese empire; what navigable river joins itself to Lara; what census of the year five was taken at Klagenfurt; also how to draw nereids neatly draped, to spin glass, stuff birds, and model flowers in wax. For the aunt liked a woman to be womanly. Of an evening she did cross stitch and owing to some mistake in her choice of silk, once embroidered a shepherdess with pink eyes. Under this torture of women's education the passionate Aurora exclaimed, certain women have died; others pine; a few who have, as Aurora had, 'relations with the unseen', survive, and walk demurely, and are civil to their cousins and listen to the vicar and pour out tea. Aurora herself was blessed with a little room. It was green papered, had a green carpet and there were green curtains to the bed, as if to match the insipid greenery of the English countryside. There she retired; there she read. 'I had found the secret of a garret room Piled high with cases in my father's name, Piled high, packed large, where, creeping in and out ... like some small nimble mouse between the ribs of mastodon' she read and read. The mouse indeed (it is the way of Mrs. Browning's mice) took wings and plunged for 'It is rather when We gloriously forget ourselves and plunge Soul-forward, headlong, into a book's profound, Impassioned for its beauty and salt of truth – 'Tis then we get the right good from a book'. And so she read and read; until her cousin Romney called to walk with her, or the painter Vincent Carrington 'whom men judge hardly as bee-bonneted Because he holds that paint a body well you paint a soul by implication', tapped on the window.

This hasty abstract of the first volume of *Aurora Leigh* does it of course no sort of justice; but having gulped down the original much as Aurora herself advises, soul-forward, headlong, we find ourselves in a state where some attempt at the ordering of our multitudinous impressions becomes imperative. The first of these impressions and the most pervasive is the sense of the writer's presence. Through the voice of Aurora the character, the circumstances, the idiosyncrasies of Elizabeth Barrett Browning ring in our ears. Mrs. Browning could no more conceal herself than she could control herself, a sign no doubt of imperfection in an artist, but a sign also that life has impinged upon art more than life should. Again and again in the pages we have read, Aurora the fictitious seems to be throwing light upon Elizabeth the actual. The idea of the poem, we must remember, came to her in the early forties when the relation between a woman's art and a woman's life was unnaturally close, so that it is impossible for the most austere of critics not sometimes to touch the flesh when his eyes should be fixed upon the page. And as everybody knows, the life of Elizabeth Barrett was of a nature to affect the most authentic and individual of gifts. Her mother had died when she was a child; she had read profusely and privately; her favourite brother was drowned; her health broke down; she had been immured by the tyranny of her father in almost conventual seclusion in a bedroom in Wimpole-street. But instead of rehearsing the well-known facts, it is better to read in her own words her own account of the effect they had upon her.

I have lived only inwardly [she wrote] or with *sorrow*, for a strong emotion. Before this seclusion of my illness, I was secluded still, and there are few of the youngest women in the world who have not seen more, heard more, known more, of society, than I, who am scarcely to be called young now. I grew up in the country – I had no social opportunities, had my heart in books and poetry, and my experience in reveries. My sympathies drooped to the ground like an untrained honeysuckle ... It was a lonely life, growing green like the grass around it ... Books and dream were what I lived in – and domestic life only seemed to buzz gently around, like the bees about the grass. And so time passed and passed – and afterwards, when my illness came ... and no prospect (as appeared at one time) of ever passing the threshold of one room again; why then, I turned to thinking with some bitterness ... that I had stood blind in this temple I was about to leave – that I had seen no Human nature, that my brothers and sisters of the earth were *names* to me, that I had beheld no great mountain or river, nothing in fact ... And do you also know what a disadvantage this ignorance is to my art? Why, if I live on and yet do not escape from this seclusion, do you not perceive that I labour under signal disadvantages – that I am, in a manner, as a *blind poet*? Certainly, there is compensation to a degree. I have had much of the inner life, and from the habit of self-consciousness and self-analysis, I make great guesses at Human nature in the main. But how willingly I would as a poet exchange some of this lumbering, ponderous, helpless knowledge of books, for some experience of life and man, for some ...

She breaks off with three little dots, and we may take advantage of her pause, to turn once more to *Aurora Leigh*.

What damage had her life done her as a poet? A great one, we cannot deny. For it is clear as we turn the pages of *Aurora Leigh*, or of the Letters – one often echoes the other – that the mind which found its natural expression in this swift and chaotic poem about real men and women was not the mind to profit by solitude. A lyrical, a scholarly, a fastidious mind might have used seclusion and solitude to perfect its powers. Tennyson asked no better than to live with books in the heart of the country. But the mind of Elizabeth Barrett was lively and secular and satirical. She was no scholar. Books were to her not an end in themselves but a substitute for living. She raced through folios because she was forbidden to scamper on the grass. She wrestled with Aeschylus and Plato because it was out of the question that she should argue about politics with live men and women. Her favourite reading as an invalid was Balzac and George Sand and other 'immortal improprieties' because 'they kept the colour in my life to some degree'. Nothing is more striking when at last she broke the prison bars than the fervour with which she flung herself into the life of the moment. She loved to sit in a café and watch people passing; she loved the arguments and politics and strife of the modern world. The past and its ruins, even the past of Italy and Italian ruins, interested her much less than the theories of Mr. Hume the medium, or the politics of Napoleon, Emperor of the French. Italian pictures, Greek poetry roused in her a clumsy and conventional enthusiasm in strange contrast with the original independence of her mind when it applied itself to actual facts.

Such being her natural bent it is not surprising that even in the depths of her sick room her mind turned to modern life as a subject for poetry. She waited, wisely, until her escape had given her some measure of knowledge and proportion. But it cannot be doubted that the long years of seclusion had done her irreparable damage as an artist. She had lived shut off, guessing at what was outside, and inevitably magnifying what was within. The loss of Flush, the spaniel, affected her as the loss of a child might have affected another woman. The tap of ivy on the pane became the thrash of trees in a gale. Every sound was enlarged, every incident exaggerated, for the silence of the sick room was profound and the monotony of Wimpole-street was intense. When at last she was able to 'rush into drawing-rooms and the like and meet face to face without mask the Humanity of the age and speak the truth of it out plainly', she was too weak to stand the shock. Ordinary daylight, current gossip, the usual traffic of human beings left her exhausted, ecstatic and dazzled into a state where she saw so much and felt so much that she did not altogether know what she felt or what she saw.

Aurora Leigh, the novel-poem, is not, therefore, the masterpiece that it might have been. Rather it is a masterpiece in embryo; a work whose genius floats diffused and fluctuating in some pre-natal stage waiting the final stroke of creative power to bring it into being. Stimulating and boring, ungainly and eloquent, monstrous and exquisite, all by turns, it overwhelms and bewilders; but, nevertheless, it still commands our interest and inspires our respect. For it becomes clear as we read that, whatever Mrs. Browning's faults, she was one of those rare writers who risk themselves adventurously and disinterestedly in an imaginative life which is independent of their private lives and demands to be considered apart from personalities. Her 'intention' survives; the interest of her theory redeems much that is faulty in her practice. Abridged and simplified from Aurora's argument in the fifth book, that theory runs something like this. The sole work of poets, she said, is to present their own age, not Charlemagne's. More passion takes place in drawing-rooms than at Roncesvalles with Roland and his knights. 'To flinch from modern varnish, coat or flounce, Cry out for togas and the picturesque, Is fatal – foolish too.' For living art presents and records real life, and the only life we can truly know is our own. But what form, she asks, can a poem on modern life take? The drama is impossible, for only servile and docile plays have any chance of success. Moreover, what we (in 1846) have to say about life is not fit for 'boards, actors, prompters, gaslight, and costume; our stage is now the soul itself'.

What then can she do? The problem is difficult, performance is bound to fall short of endeavour; but she has at least wrung her life-blood on to every page of her book, and, for the rest, 'Let me think of forms less, and the external. Trust the spirit ... Keep up the fire and leave the generous flames to shape themselves.' And so the fire blazed and the flames leapt high.

The desire to deal with modern life in poetry was not confined to Miss Barrett. Robert Browning said that he had had the same ambition all his life. Coventry Patmore's 'Angel in the House' and Clough's 'Bothie' were both attempts of the same kind and preceded *Aurora Leigh* by some years. It was natural enough. The novelists were dealing triumphantly with modern life in prose. *Jane Eyre*, *Vanity Fair*, *David Copperfield*, *Cranford*, *The Warden*, *Scenes from Clerical Life*, *Richard Feverel* all trod fast on each other's heels between the years 1847 and 1860. The poets may well have felt, with Aurora Leigh, that modern life had an intensity and a meaning of its own. Why should these spoils fall solely into the laps of the prose writers? Why should the poet be forced back to the remoteness of Charlemagne and Roland, to the toga and the picturesque, when the humours and tragedies of village life, drawing-room life, club life, and street life all cried aloud for celebration? It was true that the old form in which poetry had dealt with life – the drama – was obsolete; but was there none other that could take its place? Mrs. Browning, convinced of the divinity of poetry, pondered, seized as much as she could of actual experience, and then at last threw down her challenge to the Brontës and the Thackerays in nine books of blank verse. It was in blank verse that she sang of Shoreditch and Kensington; of my aunt and the vicar, of Romney Leigh and Vincent Carrington, of Marian Erle and Lord Howe, of fashionable weddings and drab suburban streets, and bonnets and whiskers and railway trains. The poet can treat of these things, she exclaimed, as well as of knights and dames, moats and drawbridges and castle courts. But can they? Let us see what happens to a poet when he poaches upon a novelist's preserves and gives us not an epic or a lyric but the story of many lives that move and change and are inspired by the interests and passions that are ours in the middle of the reign of Queen Victoria.

In the first place there is the story; a tale has to be told, and the poet must somehow convey to us the necessary information that his hero has been asked out to dinner. This is a statement that a novelist would convey as quietly and prosaically as possible; for example, 'While I kissed her glove in my sadness, a note was brought saying that her father sent his regards and asked me to dine with them next day'. That is harmless. But the poet has to write:

> While thus I grieved, and kissed her glove,
>> My man brought in her note to say,
> Papa had bid her send his love,
>> And would I dine with them next day!

Which is absurd. The simple words have been made to strut and posture and take on an emphasis which makes them ridiculous. Then again, what will the poet do with dialogue? In modern life, as Mrs. Browning indicated when she said that our stage is now the soul, the tongue has superseded the sword. It is in talk that the high moments of life, the shock of character upon character, are defined. But poetry when it tries to follow the words on people's lips is terribly impeded. Listen to Romney in a moment of high emotion talking to his old love Marian about the baby she has borne to another man:

> May God so father me, as I do him,
> And so forsake me, as I let him feel
> He's orphaned haply. Here I take the child
> To share my cup, to slumber on my knee,
> To play his loudest gambol at my foot,
> To hold my finger in the public ways ...

and so on. Romney, in short, rants and reels like any of those Elizabethan heroes whom Mrs. Browning had warned so imperiously out of her modern living-room.

Blank verse has proved itself the most remorseless enemy of living speech. Talk tossed up on the surge and swing of the verse becomes high, rhetorical, impassioned; and as talk, since action is ruled out, must go on all the time, the reader's mind stiffens and glazes under the monotony of the rhythm. Following the lilt of her rhythm rather than the emotions of her characters, Mrs. Browning is swept on into generalization and declamation. Forced by the nature of her medium, she ignores the slighter, the subtler, the more hidden shades of emotion by which a novelist builds up touch by touch a character in prose. Change and development, the effect of one character upon another – all this is abandoned. The poem becomes one long soliloquy, and the only character that is known to us and the only story that is told us are the character and story of Aurora Leigh herself.

Thus, if Mrs. Browning meant by a novel-poem a book in which character is closely and subtly revealed, the relations of many hearts laid bare, and a story unfalteringly unfolded, she failed completely. But if she meant rather to give us a sense of life in general, of people who are unmistakably Victorian, wrestling with the problems of their own time, all brightened, intensified, and compacted by the fire of poetry, she succeeded. Aurora Leigh, with her passionate interest in social questions, her conflict as artist and woman, her longing for knowledge and freedom, is the true daughter of her age. Romney, too, is no less certainly a mid-Victorian gentleman of high ideals who has thought deeply about the social question, and has founded, unfortunately, a phalanstery in Shropshire. The aunt, the antimacassars, and the country house from which Aurora escapes are real enough to fetch high prices in the Tottenham Court Road at this moment. The broader aspects of what it felt like to be a Victorian are seized as surely and stamped as vividly upon us as in any novel by Trollope or Mrs. Gaskell.

And indeed if we compare the prose novel and the novel-poem the triumphs are by no means all to the credit of prose. As we rush through page after page of narrative in which a dozen scenes that the novelist would smooth out separately are pressed into one, in which pages of deliberate description are fused into a single line, we cannot help feeling that the poet has outpaced the prose writer. Her page is packed twice as full as his. Characters, too, if they are not shown in conflict but snipped off and summed up with something of the exaggeration of a caricaturist, have a heightened and symbolical significance which prose with its gradual approach cannot rival. The general aspect of things, market, sunset, scenes in church, owing to the compressions and elisions of poetry have a brilliance and a continuity which mock the prose writer and his slow accumulations of careful detail. For these reasons *Aurora Leigh* remains, with all its imperfections, a book that still lives and breathes and has its being. And when we think how still and cold the plays of Beddoes or of Sir Henry Taylor lie, in spite of all their beauty, and how seldom in our own day we disturb the repose of the classical dramas of Robert Bridges, we may suspect that Elizabeth Barrett was inspired by a flash of true genius when she rushed into the drawing-room and said that here, where we live and work, is the true place for the poet. At any rate, her courage was justified in her own case. Her bad taste, her tortured ingenuity, her floundering, scrambling and confused impetuosity have space to spend themselves here without inflicting a deadly wound, while her ardour and abundance, her brilliant descriptive powers, her shrewd and caustic humour, infect us with her own enthusiasm. We laugh, we protest, we complain of a thousand absurdities, but – and this, after all, is a great tribute to a writer – we read to the end enthralled. The best compliment that we can pay *Aurora Leigh*, however, is that it makes us wonder why it has left no successors. Surely the street, the drawing-room, are promising subjects; modern life is worthy of the muse. But the rapid sketch which Elizabeth Barrett Browning flung off when she rushed into the drawing-room and met face to face the humanity of her age remains unfinished. The conservatism or the timidity of poets still leaves the chief spoils of modern life to the novelist. We have no novel-poem of the age of George the Fifth.

The Captain's Death Bed

The Captain lay dying on a mattress stretched on the floor of the boudoir room; a room whose ceiling had been painted to imitate the sky, and whose walls were painted with trellis work covered with roses upon which birds were perching. Mirrors had been let into the doors, so that the village people called the room the 'Room of a Thousand Pillars' because of its reflections. It was an August morning as he lay dying; his daughter had brought him a bunch of his favourite flowers – clove pinks and moss roses; and he asked her to take down some words at his dictation:

> 'Tis a lovely day [he dictated] and Augusta has just brought me three pinks and three roses, and the bouquet is charming. I have opened the windows and the air is delightful. It is now exactly nine o'clock in the morning, and I am lying on a bed in a place called Langham, two miles from the sea on the coast of Norfolk ... To use the common sense of

the word [he went on] I am happy. I have no sense
of hunger whatever, or of thirst; my taste is not
impaired ... After years of casual, and latterly,
months of intense thought, I feel convinced that
Christianity is true ... and that God is love ... It is
now half-past nine o'clock. World, adieu.

Early in the morning of August 9, 1848, just about dawn,
he died.

But who was the dying man whose thoughts turned to
love and roses as he lay among his looking-glasses and his
painted birds? Singularly enough, it was a sea captain;
and still more singularly it was a sea captain who had
been through the multitudinous engagements of the
Napoleonic wars, who had lived a crowded life on shore,
and who had written a long shelf of books of adventure,
full of battle and murder and conquest. His name was
Frederick Marryat. Who then was Augusta, the daughter
who brought him the flowers? She was one of his eleven
children; but of her the only fact that is now known to the
public is that once she went ratting with her father and
seized an enormous rat – 'You must know that our
Norfolk rats are quite as large as well-grown guinea pigs'
– and held on to him with her bare hands much to the
amazement of the onlookers and, we may guess, to the
admiration of her father, who remarked that his daughters were 'true game'. Then again, what was Langham?

Langham was an estate in Norfolk for which Captain Marryat had exchanged Sussex House over a glass of champagne. And Sussex House was a house at Hammersmith in which he lived while he was equerry to the Duke of Sussex. But here certainty begins to falter. Why he quarrelled with the Duke of Sussex and ceased to be his equerry; why, after an apparently pacific interview with Lord Auckland at the Admiralty, he was in such a rage that he broke a blood vessel; why, after having eleven children by his wife, he left her; why, being possessed of a house in the country, he lived in London; why, being the centre of a gay and brilliant society, he suddenly shut himself up in the country and refused to budge; why Mrs. B- refused his love and what were his relations with Mrs. S-; these are questions that we may ask, but that we must ask in vain. For the two little volumes with very large print and very small pages in which his daughter Florence wrote his life refuse to tell us. One of the most active, odd and adventurous lives that any English novelist has ever lived is also one of the most obscure.

Some of the reasons for this obscurity lie on the surface. In the first place there was too much to tell. The Captain began his life as a midshipman in Lord Cochrane's ship the *Impérieuse* in the year 1806. He was then aged fourteen. And here are a few extracts from a private log that he kept in July, 1808, when he was sixteen:

- 24th. Taking guns from the batteries.
- 25th. Burning bridges and dismantling batteries
   to impede the French.
August 1st. Taking the brass guns from the batteries.
- 15th. Took a French despatch boat off Cette.
- 18th. Took and destroyed a signal post.
- 19th. Blew up a signal post.

So it goes on. Every other day he was cutting out a brig, taking a tower, engaging gunboats, seizing prize ships or being chased by the French. In the first three years of his life at sea he had been in fifty fights; times out of number he jumped into the sea and rescued a drowning man. Once much against his will, for he could swim like a fish, he was rescued by an old bumboat woman who could also swim like a fish. Later he engaged with so much success in the Burmese War that he was allowed to bear a Burmese gilt war-boat on his arms. Clearly if the extracts from the private log had been expanded it would have swollen to a row of volumes; but how was the private log to be expanded by a lady who had presumably never burnt a bridge, dismantled a battery, or blown out a Frenchman's brains in her life? Very wisely she had recourse to Marshall's Naval Biography and to the Gazette. 'Gazette details', she remarked, 'are proverbially dry, but they are trustworthy.' Therefore the public life is dealt with dryly, if trustworthily.

The private life however remained; and the private life, if we may judge from the names of the friends he had and the money he spent and the quarrels he waged, was as violent and various in its way as the other. But here again reticence prevailed. It was partly that his daughter delayed; almost twenty-four years had passed before she wrote, and friends were dead and letters destroyed; and it was partly that she was his daughter imbued with filial reverence and with the belief also that 'a biographer has no business to meddle with any facts below the surface'. The famous statesman Sir R-- P-- therefore is Sir R-- P--; and Mrs. S-- is Mrs. S--. It is only now and then, almost by accident, that we are startled by a sudden groan – 'I have had my swing, tried and tasted everything, and I find that it is vanity'; 'I have been in a peck of troubles – domestic, agricultural, legal and pecuniary'; or just for a moment we are allowed to glance at a scene, 'You reposing on the sofa, C – sitting by you and I on the footstool' which 'is constantly recurring to my memory as a picture' and has crept into one of the letters. But, as the Captain adds, 'It has all vanished like "air, thin air"'. It has all, or almost all, vanished; and if posterity wants to know about the Captain it must read his books.

That the public still wishes to read his books is proved by the fact that the best known of them, *Peter Simple* and *Jacob Faithful*, were reprinted a few years ago in a handsome big edition, with introductions by Professor

Saintsbury and Mr. Michael Sadleir. And the books are quite capable of being read, though nobody is going to pretend that they are among the masterpieces. They have not struck out any immortal scene or character; they are far from marking an epoch in the history of the novel. The critic with an eye for pedigree can trace the influence of Defoe, Fielding and Smollett naturally asserting itself in their straightforward pages. It may well be that we are drawn to them for reasons that seem far enough from literature. The sun on the cornfield; the gull following the plough; the simple speech of country people leaning over gates, breeds the desire to cast the skin of a century and revert to those simpler days. But no living writer, try though he may, can bring the past back again, because no living writer can bring back the ordinary day. He sees it through a glass, sentimentally, romantically; it is either too pretty or too brutal; it lacks ordinariness. But the world of 1806 was to Captain Marryat what the world of 1935 is to us at this moment, a middling sort of a place, where there is nothing particular to stare at in the street or to listen to in the language. So to Captain Marryat there was nothing out of the way in a sailor with a pigtail or in a bumboat woman volleying coarse English. Therefore the world of 1806 is real to us and ordinary, yet sharp-edged and peculiar. And when the delight of looking at a day that was the ordinary day a century ago is exhausted, we are kept reading by the fact that our critical faculties enjoy whetting themselves upon a book which is not among the classics. When the artist's imagination is working at high pressure it leaves very little trace of his effort; we have to go gingerly on tip-toe among the invisible joins and complete marriages that take place in those high regions. Here it is easier going. Here in these cruder books we get closer to the art of fiction; we see the bones and the muscles and the arteries clearly marked. It is a good exercise in criticism to follow a sound craftsman, not marvellously but sufficiently endowed, at his work. And as we read *Peter Simple* and *Jacob Faithful* there can be no doubt that Captain Marryat had in embryo at least most of the gifts that go to make a master. Do we think of him as mere storyteller for boys? Here is a passage which shows that he could use language with the suggestiveness of a poet; though to get the full effect, as always in fiction, it must be read up to through the emotions of the characters. Jacob is alone after his father's death on the Thames lighter at dawn:

> I looked around me – the mist of the morning was hanging over the river ... As the sun rose, the mist gradually cleared away; trees, houses and green fields, other barges coming up with the tide, boats passing and repassing, the barking of dogs, the smoke issuing from the various chimneys, all broke upon me by degrees; and I was recalled to

the sense that I was in a busy world, and had my own task to perform.

Then if we want a proof that the Captain, for all his studiness, had that verbal sensibility which at the touch of a congenial thought lets fly a rocket, here we have a discourse on a nose.

> It was not an aquiline nose, nor was it an aquiline nose reversed. It was not a nose snubbed at the extremity, gross, heavy, or carbuncled, or fluting. In all its magnitude of proportions it was an intellectual nose. It was thin, horny, transparent, and sonorous. Its snuffle was consequential, and its sneeze oracular. The very sight of it was impressive; its sound when blown in school hours was ominous.

Such was the nose that Jacob saw looming over him when he woke from his fever to hear the Dominie breathing those strange words, 'Earth, lay light upon the lighter-boy – the lotus, the water-lily, that hath been cast on shore to die'. And for pages at a time he writes that terse springy prose which is the natural speech of a school of writers trained to the business of moving a large company briskly from one incident to another over the solid earth. Further, he can create a world; he has the power to set us in the midst of ships and men and sea and sky all vivid, credible, authentic, as we are made suddenly aware when Peter quotes a letter from home and the other side of the scene appears; the solid land, England, the England of Jane Austen, with its parsonages, its country houses, its young women staying at home, its young men gone to sea; and for a moment the two worlds, that are so opposite and yet so closely allied, come together. But perhaps the Captain's greatest gift was his power of drawing character. His pages are full of marked faces. There is Captain Kearney, the magnificent liar; and Captain Horton, who lay in bed all day long; and Mr. Chucks, and Mrs. Trotter who cadges eleven pairs of cotton stockings – they are all drawn vigorously, decisively, from the living face, just as the Captain's pen, we are told, used to dash off caricatures upon a sheet of notepaper.

With all these qualities, then, what was there stunted in his equipment? Why does the attention slip and the eye merely register printed words? One reason, of course, is that there are no heights in this level world. Violent and agitated as it is, as full of fights and escapes as Captain Marryat's private log, yet there comes a sense of monotony; the same emotion is repeated; we never feel that we are approaching anything; the end is never a consummation. Again, emphatic and trenchant as his characters are, not one of them rounds and fills to his full size, because some of the elements that go to make character are lacking. A chance sentence suggests why this should be so. 'After this we had a conversation of two hours; but what lovers say is very silly, except to themselves, and the reader need not be troubled with it.' The intenser emotions of the human race are kept out. Love is banished; and when love is banished, other valuable emotions that are allied to her are apt to go too. Humour has to have a dash of passion in it; death has to have something that makes us ponder. But here there is a kind of bright hardness. Though he has a curious love of what is physically disgusting – the face of a child nibbled by fish, a woman's body bloated with gin – he is sexually not so much chaste as prudish, and his morality has the glib slickness of a schoolmaster preaching down to small boys. In short, after a fine burst of pleasure there comes a time when the spell that Captain Marryat lays upon us wears thin, and we see through the veil of fiction facts – facts, it is true, that are interesting in themselves; facts about yawls and jolly boats and how boats going into action are 'fitted to pull with grummets upon iron thole pins'; but their interest is another kind of interest, and as much out of harmony with imagination as a bedroom cupboard is with the dream of someone waking from sleep.

Often in a shallow book, when we wake, we wake to nothing at all; but here when we wake we wake to the presence of a personage – a retired naval officer with an active mind and a caustic tongue, who as he trundles his wife and family across the Continent in the year 1835 is forced to give expression to his opinions in a diary. Sick though he was of story-writing and bored by a literary life – 'If I were not rather in want of money', he tells his mother, 'I certainly would not write any more' – he must express his mind somehow; and his mind was a courageous mind, an unconventional. The Press-gang, he thought an abomination. Why, he asked, do English philanthropists bother about slaves in Africa when English children are working seventeen hours a day in factories? The Game Laws are, in his opinion, a source of much misery to the poor; the law of primogeniture should be altered, and there is something to be said for the Roman Catholic religion. Every kind of topic – politics, science, religion, history – comes into view, but only for a fleeting glance. Whether the diary form was to blame or the jolting of a stage coach, or whether lack of book learning and a youth spent in cutting out brigs is a bad training for the reflective powers, the Captain's mind, as he remarked when he stopped for two hours and had a look at it, 'is like a kaleidoscope'. But no, he added with just self-analysis, it was not like a kaleidoscope; 'for the patterns of kaleidoscopes are regular, and there is very little regularity in my brain, at all events'. He hops from thing to thing. Now he rattles off the history of Liège; next moment he discourses upon reason and instinct; then he considers what degree of pain is inflicted upon fish by taking them with the hook; and then, taking a walk through the streets, it strikes him how very seldom you now meet with a name beginning with X. 'Rest!' he exclaims with reason; 'no, the wheels of a carriage may rest, even the body for a time may rest, but the mind will not.' And so, in an excess of restlessness, he is off to America.

Nor do we catch sight of him again – for the six volumes in which he recorded his opinion of America, though they got him into trouble with the inhabitants, now throw light upon nothing in particular – until his daughter, having shut up her Dictionaries and Gazettes, bethinks her of a few 'vague remembrances'. They are only trifles, she admits, and put together in a very random way, but still she remembers him very vividly. He was five foot ten and weighed fourteen stone, she remembers; he had a deep dimple in his chin, and one of his eyebrows was higher than the other, so that he always wore a look of inquiry. Indeed, he was a very restless man. He would break into his brother's room and wake him in the middle of the night to suggest that they should start at once to Austria and buy a chateau in Hungary and make their fortunes. But, alas! he never did make his fortune, she recalls. What with his building at Langham, and the great decoy which he had made on his best grazing land, and other extravagances not easy for a daughter to specify, he left little wealth behind him. He had to keep hard at his writing. He wrote his books sitting at a table in the dining-room, from which he could see the lawn and his favourite bull Ben Brace grazing there. And he wrote so small a hand that the copyist had to stick a pin in to mark the place. Also he was wonderfully neat in his dress, and would have nothing but white china on his breakfast table, and kept sixteen clocks and liked to hear them all strike at once. His children called him 'Baby', though he was a man of violent passions, dangerous to thwart, and often 'very grave' at home.

'These trifles put on paper look sadly insignificant', she concludes. Yet as she rambles on they do in their butterfly way bring back the summer morning and the dying Captain after all his voyages stretched on the mattress in the boudoir room dictating those last words to his daughter about love and roses. 'The more fanci-fully they were tied together the better he liked it', she says. Indeed, after his death a bunch of pinks and roses was 'found pressed between his body and the mattress'.

A Note on the Text

Virginia Woolf published selections of her critical essays, in revised form, in *The Common Reader* (first series 1925, second series 1932). The texts of all the essays gathered in this volume appear as they did on first publication in the *TLS*, barring the silent correction of typos and minor infelicities of punctuation. Their original publication dates are:

'Charlotte Brontë', April 13, 1916

'Hours in a Library', November 30, 1916

'George Eliot', November 20, 1919

'The Letters of Henry James', April 8, 1920

'John Evelyn', October 28, 1920

'On Re-reading Novels', July 20, 1922

'How It Strikes a Contemporary', April 5, 1923

'Montaigne', January 31, 1924

'Joseph Conrad', August 14, 1924

'Notes on an Elizabethan Play', March 5, 1925

'Thomas Hardy's Novels', January 19, 1928

'Fanny Burney's Half-Sister', August 29, 1930
'Aurora Leigh', July 2, 1931
'The Captain's Death Bed', September 26, 1935

TLS

Enjoyed the book?

Subscribe to the *TLS* today at just £1/$1 a week for 6 weeks.

As a *TLS* subscriber, you'll enjoy:

- The weekly *TLS* print edition, delivered straight to your door
- Full access to the *TLS* app on smartphone and tablet
- Unrestricted access to the-tls.co.uk and the *TLS* archive (going back to 1902)
- The weekly *TLS* e-newsletter
- Every *TLS* podcast

Save up to 60% today.

Go to the-tls.co.uk/VWSUB to subscribe.

Dollar currency is USD. Saving based on comparison against *TLS* Complete Works full UK subscription price. Correct at August 2019. Visit the-tls.co.uk/terms for full T&Cs.

Also from TLS Books

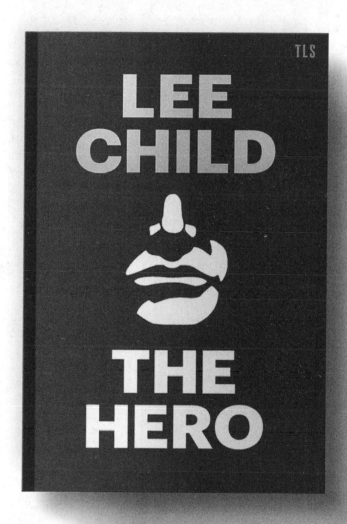

The bestselling author of the Jack Reacher
books explores what makes a hero